Praise Is His Gracious Choice

Corporate Worship Expressing Biblical Truth

Praise Is His Gracious Choice

Corporate Worship Expressing Biblical Truth

Tom J. Nettles

Praise Is His Gracious Choice
Corporate Worship Expressing Biblical Truth
Published by
Founders Press
P.O. Box 150931 • Cape Coral, FL • 33915
Phone: (888) 525-1689
Electronic Mail: officeadmin@founders.org
Website: www.founders.org
©2021 Founders Press
Printed in the United States of America
ISBN: 978-1-943539-25-3

All rights reserved. No part of this publication may be reproduced, stored in a retrieval system, or transmitted in any form by any means, electronic, mechanical, photocopy, recording or otherwise, without prior permission of the publisher, except as provided by USA copyright law.

Unless otherwise indicated, Scripture quotations are from The Holy Bible, English Standard Version® (ESV®), copyright ©2001 by Crossway, a publishing ministry of Good News Publishers. Used by permission. All rights reserved.

Scripture quotations marked NKJV taken from the New King James Version®. Copyright © 1982 by Thomas Nelson. Used by permission. All rights reserved.

Scripture quotations marked KJV taken from the King James Version of the Bible. Public domain.

Emphasis added to Scripture quotes is the author's.

Cover Design by Jaye Bird LLC

Interior Design by InkSmith Editorial Services

Contents

Preface VII

Prologue: Why Should Worship Be an Expression of Biblical Truth? 1

Section One: Theological Foundations for Worship Content

1. Salvation Is the Restoration of Praise 7
2. Spirit and Truth 21

Section Two: The New Testament Picture of Corporate Worship–God Instructs His People How to Come to Him

3. "I Was in the Spirit on the Lord's Day" 37
4. Be There And Pray 49
5. Read the Bible, Confess Its Meaning 61
6. Repentance and Remission of Sins Should Be Preached in His Name 75
7. The Congregation Sings 89
8. O Had I Jubal's Lyre 107
9. Giving 121
10. The Ordinances 133

Section Three: Coherence in Truth and Practice

11. Historic Doctrinal Definitions 153
12. Tensions That Keep Us Straight 171

Scripture Index 193

Preface

This is a book about the most important thing that a human being can do—worship the triune God. In his grace God has made a way that disobedient creatures, who have forfeited their position of free entrance into the glorious presence of God, may once again enter. It called for nothing less than infinite wisdom to devise the manner and an infinitely gracious condescension to be willing to do it. The sole mediator between God and man, the eternal Son of God who is the man Christ Jesus, paid the ransom for all who will come and worship.

It should be obvious, however, that worship of him must be in accord with his nature; he alone can describe what is acceptable worship. The sin of Adam and Eve and the murder committed by Cain arose from humans perpetrating an alternate idea of how we can know him, be like him, and please him. In ransoming his people, therefore, God has made it plain, not merely by command but by the very nature of the transaction, that we are ransomed, redeemed, forgiven, justified, and finally glorified only through the person and work of Christ. "Neither is there salvation in any other!" In accord, therefore, with that principle of God's jealousy for his name he has regulated the way in which redeemed sinners approach him in worship. Since only he knows himself fully, he alone can determine the way humans can best express their submission to him, worship of him, and love to him. That he has done so is a great grace.

This book, therefore, arises from a joyful commitment to what has been called the regulative principle of Christian worship. To paraphrase Augustine's *Confessions,* God has made us for himself and we are restless until we rest in him and are unfulfilled until we praise him in a way that accords with who he is. He has told us what is involved in this. His instructions and provisions for worship give a virtually inexhaustible expansiveness and challenge to every aspect of redeemed humanity's desire to worship and love him with all of our heart, mind, soul, and strength. Nothing good and right for that purpose is omitted; all that is idolatrous, man-centered, prone to corruption, and of vain imagination is either expressly forbidden or silently passed over. All that he has commanded we must do with all our strength. That will be satisfactory to God and will give a greater challenge to the human spirit than can be fully executed in this lifetime.

At certain places in this book, I mention "Scripture-guided worship." This is a manner of corporate worship developed by Dr. Joe Crider, Dean of the School of Church Music and Worship at Southwestern Baptist Theological Seminary. In brief the principle is this: worship must be ordered in a way that gives the greatest opportunity for a full display of all the Scripture-mandated elements of corporate worship. Historic rituals are admirable attempts to do this, but do not allow for the week-by-week scripturally and spiritually driven spontaneity of church life. In addition, in churches where the regular expository preaching of the word is emphasized, the other portions of worship frequently are not supportive of and expressive of the ideas contained in the text for the day's sermon. The principle of Scripture Guided Worship employs a biblical text parallel in thought to the sermonic text for the day. Each element of worship—prayers, confession, doctrinal affirmation, texts of music, intercession—expresses some aspect of that text selected to guide worship. It is a method that gives full sway to the Regulative Principle of worship—Scripture elements arising from a specific biblical text. At the same time the congregation is involved in giving a preparatory exposition of the sermonic text. A few examples of some elements of this principle are presented in the discussion of the different biblical elements of corporate worship.

Every aspect of this will be described—as well as defended biblically and theologically—by Dr. Crider in an upcoming book on this subject.

With that explanation, this author prays that the ideas expressed in *Praise Is His Gracious Choice* will serve to give biblical pleasure and spiritual joy in the great blessing of corporate worship.

Tom J. Nettles

Prologue

Why Should Worship Be an Expression of Biblical Truth?

By his revealed truth and eternal purpose, the Holy Spirit has led us to trust, know, love, and worship the triune God. The life of humans as described in the narratives of the Bible show that humans are fallen and in desperate need of a way out. After things began in Genesis—creation, fall, murder, infidelity, destruction, division, idolatry, promiscuity, redemptive covenant, divine faithfulness—we find that God's people need an Exodus. We need a way out of this desperate captivity to the idols of this world and the passing, but powerfully destructive, pleasures that capture our senses here. We need to be led above ourselves and above the magnetic deceit of the present into the truth of the eternal divine fellowship that we, by our sin, have forfeited.

God invades our placid destructive satisfaction with a call to turn from all that determines and deserves death. He rescues us from this by the immediate historic work of Christ and leads us to union with that once-for-all redemption by his Spirit in the context of his Truth. This is our way out.

By this union with Christ, God takes away the condemning power of sin and initiates a journey in which we escape from the debilitating, destructive, and corrupting power of sin. In the truth of God—the Bible—we are taught how to adore and what is indeed adorable in our saving God. As Scripture more and more invades the recesses of our dark minds and alters the perverse attitudes and affections of our hearts, we find the operations of the Spirit more delightful and more desirable for an ever-increasing holiness. Idols fall away and the service and worship of God is the very definition of joy.

One of the most important aspects of finding our way out of darkness into his marvelous light is the experience of corporate worship with fellow pilgrims. God joins us with others that we might be of one mind, have the same love, believe the same truth, speak with one voice as we worship the one God. Contrary to our past way of living, we do not make a god of or unto ourselves; nor do we come to him in a way contrived by our own misled and self-driven perceptions. We know him as he has revealed himself and we worship him as he requires. He revealed his truths and inspired his selected penmen to preserve that revelation so we would know our sin, know our Savior, know our brothers, and know how to know God and worship him in the full light of truth. As we walk together with our fellow pilgrims finding together the narrow way that leads to life, we are energized by the Spirit and guided by Scripture.

Besides the commands that come to each individual concerning the practice of holiness (e.g. Psalm 1; Philippians 4:4-9; 1 Thessalonians 4:1-8), God gives several specific commands of deep ethical importance that are carried out most pertinently in the body of the church (e.g. 1 Thessalonians 4:9-12; Ephesians 4:25-32). Beyond that, he gives several commands that are to be practiced as elements of corporate worship. We are to meet together, pray, read Scripture, confess the faith once-for-all given to the saints, hear preaching, give for the support of gospel proclamation and relief of the poor, teach and admonish one another through singing, practice the ordinances, confess our sins, and proclaim our love for and confidence in God's truth and his saving purpose. All of these things give growing unity and spiritual blessedness to the called-out ones who have come together to have like-minded company on our way out.

Not only do we practice all these revealed ways of reclaiming the lost holy ground, but we should practice them in a way that gives the most profound biblical order and expression to each element and shows them to be a unit in restoring us to obedience to and worship of God. The regulative principle of worship, expressed each week in accord with a text of Scripture parallel to the sermonic text, constitutes Scripture-guided worship. If the various elements of worship are regulated, would it not be edifying and wise to express these elements in a way that gives expression to a particular passage of Scripture? Such a practice gives coherence to the entire experience of corporate worship through the medium of biblically suggested order. Based on the consistency of Scripture and the analogy of faith, Scripture-guided worship sets every element of worship within a coherent biblical framework and serves as a co-exposition for the sermonic text. When we listen to the sermon, we hear the word (Romans 10:14-17); when we embrace the regulative principle, we conform to the word (1 Corinthians 14:36-38); when we worship together by the Scripture-guided text, we express the word (Colossians 3:16, 17).

I pray that you will find this idea, as it has been for me, enriching spiritually, serviceable practically, and profoundly submissive to Scripture in its overall impact. This approach to corporate worship—expressing the regulative principle through Scripture-guided worship—is highly accessible. Churches of all sizes, all levels of staff size, or lay worship leaders may form worship services of unending variety but always regulated by biblical authority. Investigate these pages and contemplate whether this is a biblically sound way to maintain gospel-focused, Christ-centered worship at the heart of the weekly gathering of the body. As fellow-pilgrims on the way out of this world to the city that cannot be shaken where the immutable and inexhaustibly glorious triune God dwells in uncreated splendor, you are invited to enrich the journey through Scripture-guided worship.

Tom J. Nettles

Section One

Theological Foundations for Worship Content

Chapter One

Salvation Is the Restoration of Praise

"Praise the Lord; Praise the Lord, O my soul. I will praise the Lord as long as I live."
Psalm 146: 1, 2

At choir practice one evening, when rehearsal focused on the arrangement of "Come Christians, Join to Sing," a teenage girl asked, "What does the phrase mean, 'Praise is his gracious choice?'" Ah, the provocative power of a well-stated poetic exclamation. Without going into the answers given on the spot at that time, I would like to affirm that the question caused some important meditation on the idea. If we discern all that is involved in a full answer to that question, we have unlocked the depths of worship.

It is Fitting to Praise God

There is no more fitting response to God than praise. We love to praise that which is beautiful, talented, pleasing, well-formed, and has some transcendent quality. Cars, athletes, foods, faces, physiques, harmony, melody, visual arts all evoke certain kinds of delight. Friendship, loyalty, reliability, unerring honesty, unalloyed kindness, tested maturity, brave virtue, wisdom—these traits of goodness and exalted character are admired and, in the best sense of the term, coveted. The apostle Paul summarized the impetus to praise in writing, "Finally, brothers, whatever is true, whatever is honorable, whatever is just, whatever is pure, whatever is lovely, whatever is commendable, if there is any excellence, if there is anything worthy of praise, think about these things" (Philippians 4:8). The life of meditation, mental and spiritual exercises that form godly character, focus on that which is "worthy of praise."

Charles Spurgeon (1834-1892) in his *Treasury of David*, giving exposition to the 135th Psalm, expressed the fitness of praise through singing:

> Yea with our best thoughts, and words, and hymns let us glorify his name. '*Sing praises unto his name; for it is pleasant.*' The adjective may apply to the singing and to the name--they are both pleasant. The vocal expression of praise by sacred song is one of our greatest delights. We were created for this purpose, and hence it is a joy to us. It is a charming duty to praise the lovely name of our God. All pleasure is to be found in the joyful worship of Jehovah; all joys are in his sacred name as perfumes lie slumbering in a garden of flowers. The mind expands, the soul is lifted up, the heart warms, the whole being is filled with delight when we are engaged in singing the high praises of our Father, Redeemer, Comforter. When in any occupation goodness and pleasure unite, we do well to follow it up without stint.

Nothing, indeed, is more appropriate for the Creator to expect of his creatures than praise, for as Spurgeon wrote,

"We were created for this purpose." "Praising God is pleasure," Spurgeon noted; "Laboring for Him is the highest bliss a mortal can know. Oh, how sweet it must be to sing His praises and never feel that the throat is dry!"[1]

We all heartily and truly sing, "All creatures of our God and King, lift us your voice and with us sing . . . O praise Him!" All beauty should lead one to expect a singular beauty that consists of absolute moral perfection. In a fallen world, however, we fail to infer moral symmetry as an absolute and infinite reality. In fact, we even find ways to resist the clear evidence for the existence of a Creator having sufficient power and intelligence to produce the natural order. Jonathan Edwards (1703-1758) considered the beauty of the world as a sure indication of holiness as the consummate and all-embracing beauty. Were the heart not manacled by sin such a response should be obvious to mind and heart. "Holiness is a most beautiful and lovely thing," even "the highest beauty and amiableness, vastly above all other beauties." It is "too high a beauty for any creatures to be adorned with," but when present in the soul it makes it "a little sweet and delightful image of the blessed Jehovah."

As Edwards contemplated the relation between the beauty and harmony of nature as coming from a holy God and as analogous to how such holiness should affect the human soul, he painted a verbal portrait of the beauty of holiness.

> It makes the soul like a delightful field of garden planted by God, with all manner of pleasant flowers growing in the order in which nature has planted them, that is all pleasant and delightful, undisturbed, free from all the noise of man and beast, enjoying a sweet

---

1 MTP, 45:sermon #2607 "Foretastes of the Heavenly Life."

calm and the bright, calm, and gently vivifying beams of the sun forever: there the sun is Jesus Christ; the blessed beams and calm breeze, the Holy Spirit; the sweet and delightful flowers, and the pleasant shrill music of the little birds, are the Christian graces.[2]

Everything in all creation lifts its voice, as it were, in its presentation of the infinite glory and wise arrangement of every particle brought into being by the God who created all things. Birds and brooks, lions and lambs, stars and stones, elephants and eggs, rhinos and rabbits, magnets and mice, bitumen and beeswax, clouds and clods all join their peculiar qualities to imply praise. In light of the complex arrangement of atoms and molecules and elements that make them what they are, they virtually have a voice to say, "A God created me." Surely it is true that "Day unto day utters speech, and night unto night reveals knowledge. There is no speech nor language where their voice is not heard" (Psalm 19:2, 3 NKJV). So clear is the truth that this is what we should hear from created things that the psalmist personifies them in the exhortation, "Let heaven and earth praise Him, the seas and everything that moves in them" (Psalm 69:34 NKJV). How strange, that as his image-bearers, we have lost the moral ability to draw such conclusions; His praise is not on our lips.

The rational order of angels and men also shows the greatness of their Creator, and not only by the purposeful arrangement of all their parts, but in their capacity to use their intelligence, their senses, their intuitional powers, and the gift of language to praise. Fallen angels know God well, but every aspect of the excellent intelligence given them in their creation sets itself in opposition to his praiseworthiness

---

[2] Yale *Works of Jonathan Edwards*, 13:163, 164.

and opposition to the truth (2 Corinthians 4:4). They will not praise him. One of the most ominous aspects of their expulsion from heaven is that they are shut off from the experience of the ineffable loveliness of eternal holiness and goodness and, thus, will never, ever, sense the urge to praise the triune God. Satan and his fellows are liars; they will remain liars; they are murderers; they will remain murderers. They are deceivers; they will remain deceivers; they are unjust, and will be unjust still; they are filthy, and will be filthy still. Nothing comes from the arch-deceiver's lips or from the lips of those whom he empowers but words of vilest blasphemy—"Then he opened his mouth in blasphemy against God, to blaspheme His name" (Revelation 13:6 NKJV). No grace will be given them to restore the praise of God to their lips. Imagine the doom and horror of seeing nothing better than themselves, nothing to draw forth admiration to any being other than their wretched selves.

WE ARE UNFIT TO PRAISE GOD

Humans are now born with a punitive corruption that dominates their spirit, senses, and intellect. Like the heavens and the earth and all created things, however, image-bearers cannot help but show forth the greatness and praiseworthiness of God, for, indeed, we are "skillfully wrought" and "fearfully and wonderfully made" (Psalm 139:14, 15). Every natural part of every created being, including Satan and his fallen cohorts, manifests the infinite power, beauty, goodness, intelligence, and consummate holiness of their Creator by their simple being, even though such praise is not volitionally given. So it will be with the saints in heaven who without ceasing praise such all-consuming holy love. God will find delight, not only in that which in the moment flows from their glorified tongues and purified spirits, but in the as yet unmanifested praise-in-potential of which his image in them is capable as they increase in capacity throughout eternity. He finds pleasure in the knowledge that his redeemed image-bearers will yet praise him, for he has made them capable of such perceptions of true glory and of ever-expanding manners of expression within which this praise will be couched. The water of life flows from the throne of God and of the Lamb giving unending nurture to the "tree of life with its twelve kinds of fruit, yielding its fruit each month." In accordance with this continued provision of grace, healing comes to the nations, nothing there is accursed, and "his servants will worship him" (Revelation 22:1-5). The continued flowing of the "river of the water of life" with the ongoing fruitfulness of the tree of life shows the ever-expanding nature of the saints' worship as they without ceasing experience the glory of "God and of the Lamb." The extrinsic praise given volitionally through present capacities always is supplemented by the intrinsic potential of each created-and-redeemed nature.

> Redemption, therefore, forms the key to the renewal of purposeful praise. Presently, fallen creatures give themselves to the will of Satan in matters concerning God in denying the infinite beauty, excellence, and desirability of God's holiness. As a result, these fallen creatures are subject to the god of this age and easily duped by his wiles. At the highest level of their resistance to the glory that is present all around them and in them, they may be called the children of the devil—like him murderers, liars, and blasphemers (John 8:37-44). Because they did not receive a love of the truth, but instead embraced the deception of

the lawless one, "God will send them strong delusion, that they should believe the lie" and thus be condemned as those who take no pleasure in truth but in unrighteousness (2 Thessalonians 2:9-12).

This sinful condition shuts us off from the most exalted use of mind and tongue. Anselm contemplated the loss involved in the fall of man and lamented:

> O pitiful lot of man, who has lost that for which he was made! O hard and frightful Fall! Alas, what he has lost and what he has found! What has departed from him and what has remained! He has lost the blessedness for which he was made, and has found the misery for which he was not made. That without which nothing is happy has deserted him, and that which by itself is nothing but misery has remained.[3]

We have been given senses so that we might internalize the experiences gained through them and relish the inward reality to which they witness in the material world. These should develop that intuitive sense of the wholeness, simplicity, and unity of the true goodness of God and flow out in praise, endless and inexhaustible, to Him who made us in his image. Instead the smog of our corrupt inwardness presses our sense to worship and serve the creature rather than the Creator.

We have lost the moral capacity to see the transcendent implication of light and color as but faint reflections of the beauty of God. A touch of hardness does not lead us to adore divine steadfastness and the feel of softness does not make us desire all of our comforts in God alone. A flood of melody and harmony leads us to cold analysis of numbers of sound waves and their relations without, at the same time, causing

---

3 Anselm, *Proslogion*, Chapter 1.

us to marvel in how God shows us that dissonance and resolution, simple melody and lush harmony demonstrate the final beauty of the multiple and complex manifestations of his perfect unity and simplicity. Taste, which lets us know how pleasant our necessary food is, seldom, if ever, leads us to the knowledge that our life, which depends on the will of God at every moment, also finds its eternal sustenance in the endless pleasure of tasting and seeing that the Lord is good. Smell, that delicate sense shows us that the things that sustain life and give it beauty (such as the aroma of food and flowers), spread their fragrance all around to show that we can never escape the presence of God, and his laudable attributes interpenetrate every space we occupy and every moment we live. We finally must confess, "But the senses of my soul have been frozen and stupefied and blocked up by the ancient enfeeblement of sin."[4]

FITNESS TO PRAISE MUST BE RESTORED

The psalmist looked at the salvation wrought by the Messiah as a restoration of praise. As we were made "very good" in the image of God, a restored knowledge of the infinite goodness *in God* of all those highest aspirations of soul *in us,* naturally produces praise. Joyful praise expresses a continual and spirit-saturated desire for fellowship with the infinitely excellent Divine Being. "Let your salvation, O God, set me up on high. I will praise the name of God with a song and will magnify him with thanksgiving" (Psalm 69:29, 30). To what then does the salvation that God gives restore us? It restores us to a position in which the highest privilege of the creature becomes the natural response of his heart—knowledgeable

---

4 Anselm, chapter 17

praise of his Creator. Another psalmist embraced with fervency of soul the relation between the beauty of God and his praiseworthiness when he wrote,

> "How lovely is your dwelling place, O Lord of hosts!
> My soul longs, yes, faints for the courts of the Lord;
> my heart and flesh sing for joy to the living God.
> Blessed are those who dwell in your house,
> ever singing your praise!"
> (Psalm 84:1, 2, 4).

Commenting on that psalm, Matthew Henry noted, "If there be a heaven upon earth, it is in praising God, in continually praising him."[5] As the prophet Isaiah was led by divine revelation to deeper knowledge of the purpose of God's sovereignty as a redeemer (Isaiah 43), he heard the Lord himself declare the end of his saving intervention (verses 19-21):

> "Behold, I am doing a new thing;
> Now it springs forth, do you not perceive it?
> I will make a way in the wilderness and rivers in the desert,
> The wild beasts will honor me,
> The jackals and the ostriches,
> For I give water in the wilderness, rivers in the desert,
> To give drink to my chosen people,
> The People whom I formed for myself
> That they might declare my praise."

PRAISE IS HIS GRACIOUS CHOICE

Praise, therefore, is his gracious choice. No sinner deserves to have such a restoration. His grace, nevertheless, abounds to us for this very purpose, that we might be restored to such a sight and experience of his goodness that the praise of his

---

5 Matthew Henry, *Matthew Henry's Commentary on the Whole Bible* (McLean, VA: MacDonald Publishing House, [1970?]) 3:558.

attributes becomes the occupation of our lives. Paul prayed, therefore, in this way: "And this I pray, that your love may abound still more and more in knowledge and all discernment, that you may approve the things that are excellent, that you may be sincere and without offense till the day of Christ, being filled with the fruit of righteousness which are by Jesus Christ, to the glory and praise of God" (Philippians 1:9-11 NKJV).

Paul's reference to the "day of Christ" in the context of our living to the "glory and praise of God" shows that praise is the "fruit of righteousness" and is our eternal occupation. The writer of Psalm 146 calls others to praise for this very reason. While there are some activities to which we have no right to call others, the praise of "Yah" is a duty intrinsic both to our status as his creatures and to his character as infinitely praiseworthy. While we have breath, we call on others to praise the Lord. We glory in his truth and commend it to others; we discern the lavish advantages of his mercy, and seek to inculcate in others that sense of dependent gratitude; we are kept from a deserved judgment in order to seek him while he may be found, and urge the quest on others.

Then the psalmist calls on himself ("O my soul!") to praise. He does not call others to an intrinsic duty to which he does not admonish his own soul. Though the psalmist himself is a prince or gifted leader, he recognizes that all he has is from the Lord, and he does not exempt his own soul from seeking to express the purest and most knowledgeable praise possible. We must often chide ourselves for our lack of fitting response to God and urge ourselves on in this most blessed, because graciously restored, of all privileges—to know and praise the Lord. Before his grace reached us, we were unfit to praise and found the duty reprehensible. His grace has shined in our hearts and opened our eyes to see the loveliness and holiness which we could not see and could not love (2 Corinthians 4:6). Having been restored to praise, let us urge our souls to this most fulfilling and eternally expanding occupation.

"I will praise the Lord as long as I live" (Verse 2). God is worthy of our praise in every conscious moment of our present life. While we live here, nothing transcends praise as a high calling for creatures made in God's image. We have many things that fall within the realm of duty and stewardship that occupy energy and time, but none of them excludes praise to God while in their doing. Whether we eat, drink, or whatever we do, do all to the glory of God (1 Corinthians 10:31).

"I will sing praises to my God while I have my being" means that the chorus of praise will never end. Psalm 145 ended, "My mouth will speak the praise of the Lord, and let all flesh bless His holy name forever and ever." Psalm 146 ends (10), "The Lord will reign forever, your God O Zion, to all generations. Praise the Lord!" The book of Revelation paints verbal pictures of scenes in which God is praised for his wisdom in creation and providence (4:9-11), his mercy in redemption (5:9, 10, 12, 13), his perfect equity in judgment (11:16-19), and his glory in wrath (15:3, 4; 16:5-7). We join the endless exultation of praise for ever and ever.

A Pastor's Perspective

Charles Spurgeon (1834-1892) saw clearly how conversion renewed the propensity of God's image bearer to praise his Maker. "When sin is pardoned, our greatest sorrow is ended, and our truest pleasure begins," Spurgeon taught. "Such is the joy which the LORD bestows upon His reconciled ones, that it overflows and fills all nature with delight. The material world has latent music in it, and a renewed heart knows how to bring it out and make it vocal." He continued, teasing out the idea of the praise implicit within the ordered universe.

> Creation is the organ, and a gracious man finds out its keys, lays his hand thereon, and wakes the whole system of the universe to the harmony of praise. Mountains and hills, and other great objects, are, as it were, the bass of the chorus; while the trees of the wood, and all things that have life, take up the air of the melodious song.

> When sinners are converted, their hearts are tuned to sing his praise. The chorus, consequently, expands among the redeemed. Unity of heart in the common adoration of a saving God enriches each individual in purity of praise and increases its dimensions exponentially.

> When God's Word is made to prosper among us and souls are saved, then everything seems full of song. When we hear the confessions of young believers and the testimonies of well-instructed saints, we are made so happy that we must praise the LORD, and then it seems as if rocks and hills and woods and fields echo our joy-notes and turn the world into an orchestra. LORD, on this happy May Day, lead me out into thy tuneful world as rich in praise as a lark in full song.[6]

DEFINING WORSHIP

Sovereign grace is given in order that unadulterated praise

---

6 Charles Spurgeon, *Cheque Book of the Bank of Faith* (Ross-shire, Scotland: Christian Focus Publications, 1996), 122.

might flow from his redeemed creatures. "He chose us in Him before the foundation of the world, that we should be holy and without blame before Him in love, having predestined us to adoption as sons by Jesus Christ to Himself, according to the good pleasure of His will, to the praise of the glory of His grace, by which he made us accepted in the Beloved" (Ephesians 1:4-6 NKJV). The redemptive blood of Christ the Beloved, covenanted by grace, not only *demonstrates* his infinite grace, but was *designed* to restore the *praise* of the glory of his grace.

We define worship, therefore, as an individual and a corporate matter. For the individual, *worship is a response of the redeemed manifested in a gracious state of increasing conformity of both understanding and affections to biblical revelation of the divine purpose in redemption through Christ. Each person moves toward a perfect state of such conformity in giving adoring submission to and seeking enjoyment in the infinite excellence of the triune God.*

All of these aspects of individual worship will, by their very nature, be expressed and nurtured in corporate worship. The additional benefit of corporate worship, as designed by God, comes in the form of gifted leadership in affirmation and instruction, mutual encouragement in the body, and unanimity in vocal expression of truth. How all of this may be sustained most edifyingly and economically in the local church composes the subject matter of this book. In that light we define corporate worship:

Corporate worship consists of *united affirmation of the infinite excellence of the triune God with a view to encouraging a grateful response to his redemptive and revelatory initiative in Christ. This involves the praise of heart and lips, the deportment of life, and corporate expressions of heartfelt repentance, transparent trust, conformity to truth, earnest hope to be like Christ, and anticipation of living eternally, body and spirit, in the glory of the presence of the triune God.*

> One thing have I asked of the Lord,
> That will I seek after:
> That I may dwell in the house of the Lord
> All the days of my life,
> To gaze upon the beauty of the Lord
> And to inquire in his temple.
> Psalm 27:4

We gaze and we inquire; we seek to heighten our affections, but always in light of more profound understanding. So shall we continue to do.

Chapter Two

Spirit and Truth

*"By the Holy Spirit who dwells within us,
guard the good deposit entrusted to you."*
2 Timothy 1:14

The worship and praise of God will not be brought into its mature state until we worship him in heaven. Then, free from all the restraints and impediments of indwelling sin which gag us here, we will worship him purely with all the other inhabitants of heaven, praising him for his creation, his works of providence, and, the crown jewel of all his works, his redemption (Revelation 4:10,11; 5:12-14). Till then, in this "already, not yet" state, we do have the "prophetic word confirmed" (2 Peter 1:19) by apostolic revelation, that to worship God rightly we worship according to the dictates of Jesus' work and words. When Peter, James, and John were "eyewitnesses of his majesty," the time in which they "beheld his glory, the glory as of the only-begotten of the Father," they also heard the word of the Father from heaven saying, "This is my beloved Son in whom I am well pleased" (2 Peter 1:17; John 1:14). Accompanying that proclamation came the command, "Hear Him!" (Matthew 17:5). True worship finds its energy and beauty in its expression of the delight that the Father has in the Son and in the central place that the Father has given the Son in his restoration of us to true praise.

The worship defined for us, therefore, in the New Testament is a christologically focused, Trinitarian worship. When the shepherds returned from having seen the child of Mary, they were "glorifying and praising God for all the things that they had seen and heard." Praise came to the lips of simple shepherds from a glimpse of the infantile glory of the incarnate Lord. When Simeon held the forty-day old child, he said, "My eyes have seen your salvation which you have prepared before the face of all peoples" (Luke 2:30, 31 NKJV). The promised salvation nestled in the hands of the grizzled old man. The wise men from the east saw the child at least several months after his birth, and when they did so, they "fell down and worshiped ." Those who knew the esteem of earthly power and glory felt no hesitance to worship this child who, at that moment, posed a threat to a king in Jerusalem. When Jesus walked on the water and stilled the storm, those in the boat "worshiped him saying, 'Truly you are the Son of God'" (Matthew 14:33). After the resurrection, as the two Marys were going to tell the disciples, Jesus greeted them and they "came up and took hold of his feet and worshiped him" (Matthew 28:9). When the disciples came to the mountain he appointed for the giving of his final commission on earth, "when they saw him they worshiped him" (Matthew 28:17).

How Jesus Defined Worship

Jesus himself established the New Testament principle of worship in his conversation with the much-married woman at the well of Samaria. He revealed to her the soon coming, and even present, change from ceremonial worship to a worship that is fulfilled and conceptually mature (John 4:19-26). No longer would the required patterns of worship be predictive and typological, but would focus on the clear knowledge of God through his redemptive grace.

To emphasize the centrality of divine revelation in worship, Jesus proclaimed the superiority of Jewish worship as a form because it was based on obedience to divine mandate and ordered its praises through a more extensive revelation. For example, Samaritans had shut themselves off from worship that would include singing the Psalm of Ethan the Ezrahite: "I will sing of the steadfast love of the Lord, forever; with my mouth I will make known your faithfulness to all generations" (Psalm 89:1). Why? It contained an extensive promise to the eternal David with whom the covenant "shall stand firm," whose seed he "will make to endure forever," and whose throne is "as the days of heaven" (Psalm 89:19-29). Going no further than the Pentateuch as the body of revealed truth and resisting the continuation of the kingship only through the line of David, they had made spiritual and doctrinal pygmies of themselves. Jesus' own judgment of these ill-informed practices was, "You worship what you do not know." That worship is acceptable which is built on truth, and that worship is the purest and greatest which expresses the most truth.

Samaritan worship was based on the fabrications instituted by Jeroboam as recorded in 1 Kings 12:25-33 and 2 Chronicles 11:13-16. To prohibit journeys to Jerusalem and thus risk the rise of disloyalty to his newly formed kingdom, Jeroboam established alternate places of worship, alternate priests, visible images (golden calves) to which offerings were made, and in general "devised in his own heart" the total fabric of worship for the people of Israel. He even made himself to be one of the priests. This led to the extermination of the house of Jeroboam "from the face of the earth" (1 Kings 13:34).

The Northern Kingdom could never overcome the invented, truncated, and arrested form of worship imagined and implemented by Jeroboam, son of Nebat. We read the refrain "He did not turn from all the sin of Jeroboam, son of Nebat, with which he made Israel to sin (2 Kings 13:4; 14:24; 15:18). The resettling of the land, therefore, resulted in syncretism and amalgamation that brought the words of Jesus to the effect, "You don't even know what you are worshiping" (2 Kings 17: 21-41; John 4: 22).

Even of Jewish worship, however, the forms would give way. In that very moment of Jesus' speaking they were being fulfilled in Christ. Worship now would be "neither in this mountain nor in Jerusalem." A designated place must give way to a perfect person. A specific location to which all worshipers worldwide must come now was to be fulfilled in a finished work, a perfectly completed moral resolution. His body, that is, his work of redemption done through his incarnation, is the temple. Its brokenness, the destruction of the temple, constituted the means of rending the temple's veil that blocked the presence of the people before a holy, unpropitiated God. (John 2:19-21; Hebrews 10:20). Now the Lord who intercedes on the basis of his perfect sacrifice, who has promised that he is with us always, who will never leave us or forsake us, who is the same yesterday and today and forever has stated new terms of worship. Wherever we find Christ's presence (where would that not be?) and his word (and where may we not read it, meditate on it, and obey it?), may be a place of worship. The ceremonies are done; the place is shattered. Now the true worshiper worships in Spirit and in truth.

The *Second London Confession* noted, "Neither prayer nor any other part of religious worship, is now under the Gospel, tied unto or made more acceptable by any place in which it is performed, or towards which it is directed; but God is to be worshipped everywhere in spirit and in truth; as in private families daily, and in secret each one by himself; so more solemnly in the public assemblies, which are not carelessly nor willfully to be neglected or forsaken when God by his word or providence calls thereunto."[1]

How does one Worship in Spirit?

Worship, so Jesus unveiled to this most unlikely of all recipients of such a pivotal and exalted revelation, would now be in Spirit and in truth. By the word "Spirit," Jesus referred to the gathering of his true Israel by the power of the Spirit according to the terms of the New Covenant. They could worship in their spirit because of the transforming operation of his Spirit. These would be given a "new spirit," removing the heart of stone for a heart of flesh. The transformation occurred by his putting "my Spirit within you" by which they would live (Ezekiel 36:26, 27; 37:14). This work would result in the writing of the law in the heart and a true experiential knowledge of God, that kind of knowledge that can be granted only by the Spirit (Jeremiah 31:33, 34). Such a standing comes with the new birth, a special operation of the Spirit of God to engender new perceptions, new affections, and to effect a new standing in those who see and enter the kingdom of God.

The Spirit also effects God's covenantal purpose by granting gifts to all those he makes members of his church. In

---
1 *Second London Confession*, XXII. 6.

instructing the Corinthians about the disciplines and spiritually appropriate employment of spiritual gifts, he affirmed that to each one is given "manifestation of the Spirit for the *profit of all*" (1 Corinthians 12:7 NKJV). Then again, near the end of this instruction he exhorted, "So with yourselves, since you are eager for manifestations of the Spirit, strive to excel in *building up the church*" (1 Corinthians 14:12). Paul wrote to the Christians of Ephesus, "To *each one of us* grace was given according to the measure of Christ's gift" (Ephesians 4:7 NKJV). These Spirit-given gifts enable corporate transformation through worship in edifying, or building up, "the *body of Christ*, until we all attain to the unity of the faith and of the knowledge of the Son of God, to mature manhood, to the measure of the stature of the fullness of Christ" (Ephesians 4:12, 13).

As the Spirit sanctifies us through the rightful use of the gifts he grants, a significant part of our transformation is the proper use of tongue and lips. If we allow the eruption of bitterness, wrath, anger, clamor, and evil speaking from our mouths, we certainly will grieve the Spirit. If, however, we learn to fill our lives and hearts with spiritual things, being thus filled with the Spirit, our lips will be employed in "addressing one another in psalms and hymns and spiritual songs, singing and making melody to the Lord with your heart, giving thanks always and for everything to God the Father in the name of our Lord Jesus Christ" (Ephesians 4:30, 31; 5:18-20). Just as surely as the content of our worship is impure without Christ, so its sincerity and transforming effect is absent without the Spirit.

Spirit and truth, therefore, constitute the whole of how true praise comes from our lips. Healthy Christian faith manifests itself in works of compassion, submission to the word of truth in its proclamation, and informed corporate worship (Hebrews 13:15-17). Joyful exhilarating worship of the sanctifying sort is at the same time mature worship, carried on in the fear of God, and with full faith that Christ, by his blood, brings us faultless to the throne of grace. "Those who serve the tabernacle," that is, who have stopped short of Jesus Christ, have "no right" to the feast of worship that resides in Christ alone (Hebrews 13:10). He suffered, humiliated before man and God, in his blood that his people surely would be sanctified, and calls us to the same humiliation before the world, but also to the eternal blessing of restored worship and praise. "Therefore, by Him let us continually offer the sacrifice of praise to God, that is, the fruit of our lips, giving thanks to His name" (Hebrews 13:12-15 NKJV).

A worship leader serves the purposes of the Spirit in worship when he looks to establish in the mouth, with the tongue, and through the lips a well-ordered, unanimous proclamation of revealed truth to the glory of Christ the Redeemer.

How Does One Worship in Truth?

"Truth" as intended by Jesus and as elucidated in the New Testament consists of a two-fold fulfillment. John 17:17-19 leads us to contemplate the power of these two distinct, but certainly complementary, perspectives.

Truth as Propositional

The first is truth in an objective, propositional sense. All the words that God has inspired are to be received as truth. To this, Jesus referred in his words, "Sanctify them in the truth; your word is truth" (John 17:17). This same meaning we find in Paul's understanding of his task in proclamation. "We refuse to practice cunning or to tamper with God's word," he wrote the Corinthians, "but by the open statement of the truth we would commend ourselves to everyone's conscience in the sight of God" (2 Corinthians 4:2). He reminded the Christians in Colossae that their salvation depended fundamentally on the sincere reception of certain propositions of truth that constituted the gospel. Of the hope laid up in heaven they had "heard before in the word of truth, the gospel." It was, precisely, from Epaphras that they "heard it, and understood the grace of God in truth." From that hearing they would be brought into the realm of Spirit and truth. They would be "filled with the knowledge of his will in all spiritual wisdom and understanding" and increase "in the knowledge of God" (Colossians 1:5-7, 9, 10).

The priority of hearing and understanding truth lay behind Paul's instructions to the Corinthians about their use of untranslated tongues. Paul pointed to the necessity of clarity in proclamation and every part of corporate worship (1 Corinthians 14:9-11). Speech, motions, or content "that is not intelligible" do not edify and, thus, constitute no part of that which God designates as worship. Attempts at non-verbal presentations are similar to speaking in tongues without an interpreter. With words I do not understand, "I will be a foreigner to the speaker and the speaker a foreigner to me" (1 Corinthians 14:11). With symbolic leaps and pirouettes, I will be a foreigner to the dancer, and the dancer a foreigner to me. With facial contortions and charade-like jerks of limbs, I will be a foreigner to the mime, and the mime a foreigner to me. With combinations of colors and depictions of places and faces, I will be a foreigner to the artist, and the artist a foreigner to me. Though the Christian worldview fosters and celebrates multifaceted manifestations of human creativity in imitation of the God in whose image we are made, corporate worship only occurs when driven at every point by purposefully and clearly proclaimed truth.

TRUTH AS CHRISTOLOGICAL

In addition to the truth of propositions, Jesus referred to truth as the clear manifestation, fulfillment, and consummation in his own person of all that had been promised. He prayed, "And for their sake *I consecrate myself*, that they also may be sanctified in truth" (John 17:19). His determined fulfillment of that which he was sent to do brought the fullness of covenantal truth into objective fulfillment and eliminated the usefulness of types and ceremonies. In this sense, we find John emphasizing Jesus as the "Truth." For sure, Jesus is the one who was "full of grace and truth" (John 1:14). In light of his words and works, we confess that "Grace and truth came through Jesus Christ" (John 1:17). On this basis, Jesus claimed exclusivity as the reconciler of fallen humanity to God when he affirmed in John 14:6, "I am the way, the truth, and the life." No other person but the one who was both God and Man, no other forgiveness than through the bearing of just wrath, no other righteousness unto life than that which he perfected, and no other presence before God than that which he attained in his resurrection can bring the vile with confidence and praise before the Father.

TRUTH CONFESSED AND SUNG

This commitment to truth in these two complementary dimensions, propositions and Person, was kept before the early church in the pregnant phraseology of confessions. In 2 Timothy 2:8, Paul summarized the gospel he preached in a simple church confession: "Remember Jesus Christ, risen from the dead, the offspring of David, as preached in my gospel". Just a few verses later another confession states:

"If we have died with him,
We will also live with him;
If we endure, we will also reign with him.
If we deny him, he also will deny us;
If we are faithless, he remains faithful,
For he cannot deny himself."

Those who have no faith, whose hope is not firmly fixed on the work of Christ, will find the world more congenial than the cross of Christ. The revelation of their faithless estate under testing will at the same time reveal the faithfulness of God to his standard of world-denying trust in the finished work of his Son. Defectors will not find him an accepting judge when all flesh appears before him. In the full range of personal and propositional truth, New Testament worship found a way to encourage and warn in the same corporate recitation.

It is instructive that the propositional truths about the Christological truth have been put before us in a hymn in 1 Timothy 3:16 named "The Mystery of Godliness." It is a short hymn of six lines summarizing how God, through Christ, secured the salvation of his people.

He was manifested in the flesh,
vindicated by the Spirit,
seen by angels,
proclaimed among the nations,
believed on in the world,
taken up in glory.

Here Paul affirmed the truth of words apparently used in the church's worship. The church is "a pillar and buttress of the truth" (1 Timothy 3:15) and its singing and confessing must reflect it. The stanza summarizes truths concerning the Lord Jesus Christ in whose person and through whose work the church came into existence. The church is his body (Ephesians 1:22, 23; 5:18; Colossians 1:18), his bride (Ephesians. 5:25 cf. Revelation 19:7) purchased with his blood (Acts 20:28). The hymn has internal rhyme created by six verbs all in the same tense (revealed, vindicated, seen, proclaimed, believed on, taken up). It has two stanzas of three lines each, the key ideas related in chiastic style. The first line speaks to when he came down from heaven, "He was manifested in the flesh." The last line emphasizes that when he went back to heaven that same flesh, glorified subsequent to his death, was "Taken up in glory."

The first stanza, therefore, begins with the incarnation, the Lord from heaven took upon himself our flesh in order to live in our nature. It affirms the presence and necessary work of the Spirit to bring him to perfected righteousness (Luke 2:52; 4:1, 2; Romans 1:4; Hebrews 9:14). The redeeming events of his life are summarized in the engaging truth that angels observed in these amazing events of the Son of God, their Master. How astounding to them that he lived among men in a nature inferior to the angelic but soon to be exalted above them. How peculiar, but wondrously godlike, that fallen creatures could be redeemed by such means, given that the angels themselves saw no redemption of their kind (1 Peter 1:12; Hebrews 1:4, 14; 2:14-16). From the announcement of the birth of John the Baptist all the way through the ascension of Christ (Luke 1:11-20; Acts 1:10, 11) and in many appearances at pivotal events in between, angels informed, announced, ministered, and observed with wonder.

The second stanza begins with the effect of Christ's appearance in his proclamation to the Gentiles. The chiasm relates the last line of the first stanza to the first line of the second stanza. It was not to angels that the task of proclaiming the gospel came but to the redeemed sinners themselves. They, the angels, saw and announced at the birth, resurrection, and ascension; redeemed, sinners preached to the nations. The second lines of both stanzas correlate. As the Spirit had vindicated Christ in his life and by his resurrection, so would he vindicate Christ in the proclamation of his life and victorious death. Though rejected during his days on earth, now, by the effectual continuation of the Spirit's commitment to the glory of Christ (John 16:14), he was "believed on in the world." By the Spirit's power, belief unto life would accompany proclamation. "Taken up in glory," they sang, affirming that his ascension marked the certainty that his work of redemption was accepted in heaven, and that by him, gifts to men had been given for the establishing of the church as the pillar and buttress of truth (Ephesians 4:8-13).

In a simple but mystifying claim, Jesus gave to the heathen Pontius Pilate, a man whose loose hold on truth was foundational to his squeamish embrace of safety, words of pure grace, "For this purpose was I born and for this purpose came I into the world, to bear witness to the truth" (John 18:37). Later that day, that witness would be sealed as he cried, "It is finished," thus becoming the "author and the finisher of faith." The man who saved his life lost it; the man who lost his life saved it.

Even so, to the nameless and scorned Samaritan woman, Jesus, responding to her knowledge that Messiah "will tell us all things," shifted the entire focus of worship and knowledge to his own person: "I who speak to you am he."

Worship, Therefore, in Spirit and Truth

The great privilege and power of worship is found in the corporate execution of biblically-driven opportunities to reflect Spirit and truth. Under the authority of Scripture and motivated by the glory of Christ, the worship leader works to duplicate the biblical model of singing and confessing the faith. From tongues employed in deceit, lips that formerly flowed with the venom of asps, and mouths that harbored curses and bitterness, the Spirit and the Truth prompt us to keep our tongues from evil and our lips from deceit, and to be a people who have learned, by the choice of his grace to praise. "You are a chosen race, a royal priesthood, a holy nation, a people for his own possession, that you may proclaim the excellencies of him who called you out of darkness into his marvelous light" (Romans 3:13, 14; 1 Peter 3:10, 2:9).

Section Two

The New Testament Picture of Corporate Worship– God Instructs His People How to Come to Him

Chapter Three

"I Was in the Spirit on the Lord's Day"

*"On the first day of the week,
when we were gathered together."*
Acts 20: 7

Revealed Truth Governs Worship

The knowledge of God comes through his active revelation through his works. His revelatory works are creation, providence, redemptive acts, and special propositional revelation. God has an eternal propensity to want to be known by other rational beings outside himself. Since he alone is self-existent, eternal, infinitely excellent in every attribute, and yet simple and undivided in his essence, other rational beings must necessarily be created by him and assigned their own relative excellence by him. Since he alone is self-existent, consists of such beauty and virtue incomprehensible by any but himself, enjoyed perfectly by none but himself (and therefore triune), he is to be the object of adoration, praise, and worship by all his creatures, a stewardship that can never be exhausted. Though all things cannot but praise him in some measure,

God will restore praise to its fullest according to his eternal purpose.

Though without rational purpose, flowers and rocks and mountains and rivers and oceans and planets and stars and tomatoes praise him in their stunning variety, their mysterious and breathtaking individual composition, and their perfectly integrated teleology. Even at the level of the inanimate and non-rational, the act of creation itself is necessarily revelatory for it expresses "his eternal power and godhead" (Romans 1:20). This gives a knowledge of God and calls us to worship.

The animate world adds an increased dimension of evidence of the praiseworthiness of the God who made such a variety (still greater than we have yet discovered) of living things. In my own backyard, I marvel at the energy, cunning, agility, relative strength, form, and instinct of robins, finches, cardinals, chipmunks, squirrels, hawks, doves, beetles, and earthworms. The sea-creatures—from ghost crabs to killer whales—can only excite awe and wonder at their quick delicate survival tactics and their overwhelming ponderance of strength and beauty. They magnify their Creator loudly even though only instinctually. They call us to a more rational and exuberant praise.

Rational beings include angels and men. Angels are either elect or fallen. Elect angels worship him constantly with a deep sense of God's holiness and an awareness and joyful willingness to keep up the chorus, "Glory to God in the Highest." Fallen angels, because they are creatures, show forth God's praise by their intelligence evidenced in their ability to scheme, to converse, to deceive. There is nothing volitional in their manifestation of God's greatness; the necessity of it is galling to them for they express undiluted hatred of God's pure holiness. That evil schemers hate God and seek to cross his purposes while holy beings praise him unceasingly should prompt us to be jubilant and exalt him for all his goodness.

All human persons are fallen. Some of the fallen are elect and some are not. All are obliged to worship, honor, obey, and praise their maker for his natural, inherent, absolute, and ineffable greatness. As discussed in the first chapter, some are restored to praise by the redemptive work of Christ. Others are justly left in their rebellion according to their own wills. Those who are restored to praise learn how to do so with clarity, purity, and increasing truthfulness by divine revelation. The Holy Spirit effects the redemptive love of Christ and the gracious purpose of God the Father in bringing the elect to a frame of mind and heart fit for praise; He also has revealed how God requires his elect, redeemed creatures to worship him. In Revelation 4 we find both creation and providence as sources of continual worship. In Revelation 5 we find the multiple dimensions of worship added by the consummation of redemption in the Lamb who was slain.

In our restoration to praise, God has graciously regulated it, that is, has given divinely revealed elements of what constitutes true worship for his redeemed people. The entire life of the Christian should be constantly infused with praise and worship. But, does God require a particular time when his people will come together and, in particular ways, give a corporate expression of humble submission and willing exaltation to him as a preview of their eternal occupation in heaven? The answer is "Yes;" the time is the Lord's Day. This time is an element of God's moral law as expressed in the Ten Commandments. Let's look briefly at this gracious provision of God.

COMMANDING A TIME

A DAY TO REMEMBER

The Sabbath commandment was given to provide a time when creatures could remember, imitate, and meditate on the rest implied by a completed work of God (Exodus 20:11), particularly in light of a redemptive action on his part (Exodus 20:1). This kind of imitation and meditation is not merely an arbitrary stipulation; it reflects an intrinsically moral principle given the relation of the Creator to creatures made in his image.

For Israel, the covenant people redeemed from slavery in Egypt, the seventh day of the week was set aside—to be kept holy, to be sanctified—for that recognition, based on God's rest from creation. During the wilderness wanderings, its dominant expression was rest from normal daily labors. Later, a major element of obedience to God was faithfulness in sanctifying the Sabbath day (Nehemiah 13:22) and in considering it a "delight" in which they rested not only from their labors and pursuit of their own pleasures, but from their own words (Isaiah 58:13, 14). In the post-exilic period the Sabbath became a time of instruction in the Scriptures. We find Jesus himself observing that practice and using it to give instruction concerning himself, the true importance of the Sabbath, and also the true meaning of Scripture (Luke 4:16-30; 6: 1-11). Paul used this settled purpose to his advantage in evangelism (Acts 17:1-4). Churches founded under apostolic labors came together on the first day of the week in recognition and celebration of the completed work of redemption as confirmed by the resurrection (1 Corinthians 16:2).

In Romans 14: 5, 6a Paul wrote that the esteeming of days concerns special observances throughout the year, whether religious or civil, in which a Christian may or may not participate without any negative reflection on the sufficiency of the gospel. Paul had in mind specifically those days as a part of the Jewish calendar that were designed to give gratitude to God for his watching over his people and providing for them. Some Jewish Christians were insistent on maintaining that rhythm of national life and were seeking to impose these on Gentile Christians. Colossians 2:16 refers to this; "Therefore no one is to act as your judge in regard to food or drink or in respect to a festival or a new moon or sabbath days."

Days That Can Be Forgotten

Certain special Sabbaths prescribed in the Old Testament were clearly irrelevant to the New Covenant community (Leviticus 23:24, 32). Some might, however, still be a matter of observance, recalling special events in the life of the nation of Israel without any denial of Christ's having fulfilled all the types and offices of the Old Covenant (e.g. Feast of Trumpets). There can be no doubt that a Christian could not go back to the sacrificial system without denying the priesthood of Christ (Hebrews 10:1-14) and thus the Sabbath connected with the Day of Atonement (Leviticus 23:32) would be necessarily abolished. Days in themselves, however, that commemorate historical events or special holidays (Acts 20:6, 16) could be observed without a denial of Christ's perfect fulfillment of the sacrifices. Some Christians feel that it is a compromise to celebrate special religious days such as Christmas or Easter and that national holidays such as the fourth of July or even Thanksgiving should not be given any special significance. One may forego celebrating these with no loss to his spiritual life. On the other hand, one may celebrate them, sanctify them, and observe them in honor of the Lord.

Paul is not talking about the day of the week for Christian worship as negotiable according to conscience. The *ESV Study Bible* on Romans 14:5 represents the thinking of many evangelicals in saying, "The weak thought some days were more important than others. Given the Jewish background here (see verse 14,) the day that is supremely in view is certainly the Sabbath. The strong think every day is the same. Both views are permissible. Each person must follow his own conscience. What is remarkable is that the Sabbath is no longer a binding commitment for Paul but a matter of one's personal conviction." It classifies the Sabbath command as a part of the ceremonial laws, "no longer binding on new covenant believers."[2]

Ironically, to impute a Sabbath commitment to weakness in "the faith" calls into question some of the most profound and edifying thinkers in the history of the Christian church. For example, the *Second London Confession* has a chapter of eight paragraphs devoted to "Religious worship and the Sabbath Day." One of its phrases says that the Sabbath "from the beginning of the world to the resurrection of Christ, was the last day of the week; and from the resurrection of Christ, was changed into the first day of the week which is called the Lord's Day; and is to be continued to the end of the world, as

---

2 That comment closes with, "However, it is still wise to take regular times of rest from work, and regular times of worship are commanded for Christians (Heb. 10: 24, 25; Acts 20:7 [!])." In Colossians 2: 17, this study Bible states, "It is debated whether the Sabbaths in question included the regular seventh-day rest of the fourth commandment, or were only the special Sabbaths of the Jewish calendar." ESV Study Bible (Wheaton, IL: Crossway Bibles, 2011).

the Christian Sabbath; the observation of the last day of the week being abolished."[3]

WHAT MAKES THE DIFFERENCE?

The Sabbath as a moral proposition was instituted at creation in recognition of God's completed work (Genesis 2:3). Divine sovereignty over creation, its goodness as a reflection of his glory in all of its levels of existence, and his perfect effecting of a covenantal purpose are all embedded within the institution of the Sabbath. It is precisely at the point of rejecting this reality within creation as enforced by regular Sabbath observance that provides the most poignant path of rebellion for fallen humanity: "For since the creation of the world His invisible attributes, His eternal power and divine nature, have been clearly seen, being understood through what has been made, so that they are without excuse." The Sabbath was given in the framework of the moral duties of man to maintain that recognition, but it quickly was ignored so that "even though they knew God, they did not honor Him as God or give thanks, but they became futile in their speculation, and their foolish hearts were darkened" (Romans 1:20, 21). From this refusal of honoring God, the formal recognition of God's creation rights, flowed increasingly perverse idolatry, sexual perversions of augmented malignity, and the breaking of all the commandments written on the heart.

The Sabbath is set within this moral framework as the fourth commandment of the Ten Commandments accompanied by reinforcements (Exodus 20:8-11). It is an insuperable

---

[3] William L. Lumpkin, Baptist Confessions of Faith (Valley Forge: The Judson Press, 1969), 282

contextual difficulty to say that the commandment would be relegated to the category of ceremonial, a commandment to be dispensed with and subjected to pure relativity by making it a matter of individual conscience. This is strikingly the case when we view its vital connection to the worship and honoring of God with a timely recognition of his ownership of the world, the world's being brought into existence for his own purpose, and as a perpetual recognition of the character of God's finished work as a manifestation of his glory.

The Sabbath was given particular covenantal status in Israel. For enforcing its close observance in order to establish the people as God's special possession, it was protected with certain civil and ceremonial requirements, even unto death (Exodus 31:14, 15; Numbers 15:32-36). Other days also were called sabbaths related to the recognition of historical events in the life of Israel (Leviticus 23:39). Others would be established in anticipation of the final Sabbath observance that would be accomplished by Christ and then recognized in perpetuity by his people (Leviticus 16:29-34). Temporary measures would be made obsolete with a new manner of identifying the people of God and moral judgments would be fulfilled as established in the life of Christ and brought to perfection by his complete work of atonement (John 2:18-22; 3:1-8; 4:21-26; Galatians 3:13, 14; Philippians 3:3).

These civil and ceremonial applications as given to Israel as a nation no longer are intrinsic to the moral import of the Sabbath. The memorial and symbolic aspect of the seventh day has been changed to the first in light of reasons given below, though the intrinsic moral principle of honoring God as sovereign and covenantally possessive of his people still stands. Also, violation does not call for capital punishment or other civil applications (Nehemiah 11:20, 21). The identity of the new community of God no longer is national or ethnic, and its impetus and means for holiness transcends the legal codes of the nations.

These fulfillments, however, of both the ceremonial and moral components of the commandments do not negate the fundamentally moral character of the fourth commandment. It is still a testimony to the covenantal faithfulness of God and the consequent claim that he has on the affections of all people, both by way of creation and of redemption.

O Perfect Redemption

Greater than the work of creation is the work of redemption. On that *fait accompli* consummated by Christ is based the entirety of the new creation, both in its people and the glory of its place (2 Peter 3:11-13). The moral nature of giving perpetual and timely recognition and worship in light of this completed work still abides. On the first day of the week, the full acceptance of Christ's work of new creation was announced by the resurrection—"declared to be the Son of God with power according to the Spirit of holiness, by the resurrection from the dead. . . . Thanks be to God, who gives us the victory through our Lord Jesus Christ" (Romans 1:4; 1 Corinthians 15:57).

If the worship of the God of creation was revealed to be of moral necessity through the commandment, how much more should redemptive grace be insinuated in that commandment as the fountain from which all true worship flows. If the foretaste of redemptive power and purpose on the part of God undergirded the Ten Commandments (Exodus 20:1, 2), then how much more does the completed work of redemption, a necessary satisfaction of the moral law, validate the holiness of that law. Faith in the promised Messiah neither weakens nor negates, but reinforces and expands, by grace and authority, the content of the time of corporate praise for God's covenant people.

We are in fact given both by example and then command the day to be set aside for all that is involved in corporate worship. The One who became a curse for us (Galatians 3:13), bought us with a price (1 Corinthians 6:20), and called us to a life of spiritual worship (Romans 12:1, 2) has transformed but not abolished the moral reality to "Remember." The church, the Israel of God bought by the cross and brought by the circumcision of heart (Galatians 6:14-16), remembers the great work of God by concrete expression of a day set aside for that purpose with all that are within the body.

Immediately, the disciples began to come together on the first day of the week (John 20:19, 26). Paul assumes that the church as a congregation is meeting together (1 Corinthians 5:4; 11:18, 20; 14:26) at some established time. That this established time is the first day is confirmed by the practice of the church at Troas (Acts 20:7 - "Now on the first day of the week when the disciples came together"). This is consistent with his instruction to the Corinthian church when he points to the "first day of the week" as the time when they would be together (1 Corinthians 16:1,2) in order to collect their offering. Unless the apostles, or the church, had assumed an unauthorized power to designate such an important aspect of the new covenant community apart from divine warrant, we can look upon the first day of the week as the time when the regulated elements of corporate church life were to be practiced.

These aspects of community spiritual life are surely commanded in Hebrews that we might encourage one another and hear the word together. If this were a simple matter of individual conscience the writer of Hebrews would not have said, "Let us consider how to stir up one another to good works, not neglecting to meet together, as is the habit of some, but encouraging one another, and all the more as you see the Day drawing near." (Hebrews 10:24, 25). If the command to meet together stands, then the day of meeting would surely conform to the stated practice of the churches and be consistent with the newly arranged sabbath rest, shifting the emphasis from creation to redemption (Hebrews 4:9, 10, 14-16).

The matter that is left to the Christian's conscience, therefore, is not a stated day of worship as an element of the moral law of God, but the ceremonial part of the observance of certain days. On that day, the Lord's Day, God graciously has told us how we may approach him and how we can gain the greatest pleasure and growth in holiness.

Chapter Four

BE THERE AND PRAY

"I urge that supplications, prayers, intercessions, and thanksgivings be made for all people."
1 Timothy 2:1

Though many individual disciplines advance growth in grace and holiness of life, none can proceed to Christian maturity apart from the corporate fellowship of the church. Gifts are supplied by the Spirit "for the edifying of the body of Christ." In that context, we come to unity in the faith. Unity makes necessary a plurality of persons moving into the sharing of the same mind and the same affection. Attaining to the "perfect man," speaking the truth in love, being joined and knit together, and the "edifying of itself in love" all come in the dynamic interaction of many people responding to the effective working of every member of the body doing its share (Ephesians 4:12-16). Only with body life do we have mature life.

For that reason, the New Testament gives both instructions and examples of what constitutes a Spirit-empowered, Christ centered, revelation-driven body in which both corporate and individual maturity thrive. How does the church become the people who, in this fallen rebellious world, show forth the praises of the one who called us from darkness to light, from death to life, from corruption to holiness, and from condemnation to justification?

MEET TOGETHER UNDER THE WORD

After the apostles were threatened not to preach the crucifixion, burial, resurrection and exclusivity of Jesus as the way of salvation, they rejoiced and returned to "their friends" and "lifted their voices together to God" (Acts 4:10-12, 21-24). When they continued even in the face of threats and were beaten for proclaiming that Jesus was exalted to the right hand of the Father to give repentance and forgiveness of sins to Israel, they rejoiced (Acts 5: 31, 40, 41). We find then that "every day in the temple and from house to house, they did not cease teaching and preaching Jesus as the Christ" (42). They suffered together and they worshiped together. At its most basic level, how do we emulate apostolic Christianity?

First, we must meet together. This clearly was the New Testament practice according to divine mandate. If we are to "stir up one another to love and good works" we cannot neglect "to meet together." Some who had fallen into a sloppy stewardship of presence put themselves and others in danger of fatal compromise with the world. We need the support and spiritual gifts of others to "hold fast the confession of our hope," avoid the pressure to deny Christ, and be strengthened by the promises of God's faithfulness. (Hebrews 10:23-25).

Only in the regularity of the corporate setting can we find the spiritual sanctification of "bearing with one another in love." Avoid all contact with brothers and sisters and lose all the benefit of patient endurance. None who isolates himself from the regular and rhythmical community life can show that he is "eager to maintain the unity of the Spirit in the bond of peace" (Ephesians 4:2, 3). James's warning, "Let every person be quick to hear, slow to speak, slow to anger," has no relevance to a person who secludes himself from hearing the word of God along with his fellow believers. Together they contemplate what is said before responding, and listen with patience and love to others, knowing that they too are under authority and must receive "with meekness the implanted word, which is able to save your souls" (James 1:19-21). It is only in the testiness of corporate life together that we are challenged to "Live in harmony with one another," by learning not to be "haughty, but associate with the lowly" (Romans 12:16). Paul longed for the benefit of the company with the Roman Christians "that we may be mutually encouraged by each other's faith, both yours and mine" (Romans 1:12).

Interestingly, the letter of Ignatius to the Ephesians in about AD 112 emphasized the necessity of assembling together under the instruction of the bishop: "Let no one be misled: if anyone is not within the sanctuary, he lacks the bread of God. For if the prayer of one or two has such power, how much more that of the bishop together with the whole church! Therefore whoever does not meet with the congregation thereby demonstrates his arrogance and has separated himself, for it is written: 'God opposes the arrogant.'"[4]

As cited before, the *Second London Confession,* as well as the *Westminster Confession of Faith*, points to the assembly as particularly important in the life of worship: "So more

---

4 Michael W. Holmes, ed., *The Apostolic Fathers*, trans. J. B. Lightfoot and J. B. Harmer, 2nd ed. (Grand Rapids: Baker Book House, 1989), 88.

solemnly in the public assemblies, which are not carelessly nor willfully to be neglected or forsaken when God by his word or providence calls thereunto."[5]

This divine mandate places on those who plan worship the stewardship of being clearly intentional in the way they set forth the authority of revealed truth over the entire congregation. It meets in the unity of truth to confess together the merciful work of the triune God in the eternal covenant of redemption. Only that work of Trinity in unity has brought together the people for the purpose of learning to express fittingly and truthfully their gratitude for and dependence on God's purpose of grace. We celebrate the *many* in the Spirit-given diversity of gifts, but always in the service of the *one*—"though many, we are one body in Christ, and individually members one of another" (Romans 12:5). From beginning to end, words spoken from the pulpit and from the pew should prompt the entire body, now assembled together for this purpose, to hear truth, meditate carefully, and respond fittingly to God's gracious disclosure. Instruction to the mind, challenge to the soul, comfort to the heart, and praise from the lips must be the effect of the community assembly or the many person-hours invested will be vainly spent.

Praying by the Word

An essential element of every meeting for corporate worship is prayer. In prayer we seek to unite in agreement on earth concerning those things that God has decreed from heaven. As a matter of conformity to biblical mandate and pattern, every meeting of corporate worship is undertaken

---

[5] William L. Lumpkin, *Baptist Confessions of Faith* (Valley Forge: The Judson Press, 1969), 282

in the spirit of prayer. Prayer in the worshiping body is an appropriate response to biblical revelation in three ways; one, we engage in it because the Bible says so; two, we fill the substance of our prayers with what the Bible says we should pray and in accord with the biblical examples of prayer; and three, prayer should express the contours and content of the Scripture passage that guides our worship.

THE BIBLE TELLS ME SO.

Bible instruction about the necessity of corporate prayer permeates the New Testament. "Be constant in prayer," Paul told the Romans (12:12). In the Corinthian church, Paul gave instructions about prayer that would allow the members of the congregation to say "Amen" to what was prayed (1 Corinthians 14:15, 16). The Ephesian church Paul instructed to give "thanks always and for everything to God the Father in the name of our Lord Jesus Christ" (Ephesians 5:20). Paul assumed that through the prayers of the church at Philippi, joined with the help of the Spirit of Jesus Christ, he would be delivered (Philippians 1:19). How revealing that the aid of the Holy Spirit, in some instances, rides upon the prayers of a united church. To the church at Colossae, Paul instructed, "Continue steadfastly in prayer, being watchful in it with thanksgiving." Prayers in the body must reflect an earnest and unwearied devotion to the grace of prayer. This is no mean privilege, to address as Father the merciful Creator, who has been propitiated by the blood of Christ given as a ransom (1 Peter 1:17-19). As our lives, so our corporate worship should proceed as in a sea of prayer. Steadfastness and watchfulness means that in prayer our minds are not sleepy and dull but active and alive to the endless stream of blessings that saturate our lives.

In the Reformed worship of Geneva, Calvin sought to model obedience to Scripture by interspersing prayers in French at specific points in the service. He included an invocation, a specific prayer for absolution and confession of sins, a prayer for illumination before the sermon, and a final prayer of intercession that concluded with a paraphrase of the Lord's Prayer. The prayer of confession began with an invitation for the congregation to present themselves before the Lord in confession "following with your heart my words."

> Lord, God, eternal and almighty Father, we confess and truly recognize, before thine holy majesty, that we are poor sinners, conceived and born in iniquity and corruption, inclined to do evil, unprofitable for all good; And that from our vice we endlessly and ceaselessly transgress thine holy commandments. So doing, we incur, by thy just judgment, ruin and perdition upon us. Nevertheless, Lord, we are displeased with ourselves for having offended against thee and condemn ourselves and our vices with true repentance, desiring that Thy grace support us in our calamity. Have pity upon us, then, God and Father, most blessed and full of mercy, in the name of thy Son, Jesus Christ our Lord. And in wiping out our vices and spots pour upon us and increase from day to day the gifts of thine Holy Spirit, in order that, recognizing our unrighteousness with all our heart we may be touched with displeasure, which engenders true repentance in us, which mortifying us in all sins, produces in us fruits of righteousness and innocence that may be agreeable to thee, by Jesus Christ our Lord. Amen.[6]

---

6 *The Piety of John Calvin: An Anthology Illustrative of the Spirituality of the Reformer*, translated and edited by Ford Lewis Battles (Grand Rapids: Baker Book House, 1978), 119.

THE BIBLE INSTRUCTS US.

Second, Scripture guides our corporate prayer by instructing us as to the content of prayer. In the apostolic era, when it was necessary for churches to be given specific guidance in both doctrinal and procedural matters, gifts of prophecy, tongues, prayer, and singing all had the element of revelation attached to them. The canon of the New Testament was in an observable, but early, stage of development, and increasingly the churches had access to the whole range of apostolic revelation (Colossians 4:16). Till its completion, however, the living apostles gave a clear range within which such revelations could operate (cf. 1 Corinthians 12:1-3; 14:36-38; 2 Corinthians 10:1-8; 11:4-6; 1 John 4:1-3, 6-7;). Worship would consist partly of the practice and exposition of the established canonical revelation, while other elements would be guided by immediately inspired songs, prophecies, prayers, and, when interpreted, speeches in other languages, either heavenly or earthly. Such revelatory insights given by the Spirit, therefore, aided in personal guidance, personal sanctification, and also instruction of the body.

Personal revelatory blessings edified and instructed the individual, and seemingly remained largely impressionistic, heightening the sense of awe of the individual recipient (1 Corinthians 14:14). For corporate worship, however, clear and comprehensible instruction and rational discourse was necessary and apostolically mandated (1 Corinthians 14:5, 15, 16). Paul insisted that all of it be addressed to the congregation in an understandable way. "I will pray with my spirit, but I will pray with my mind also . . . Otherwise, if you give thanks with your spirit, how can anyone in the position of an outsider say 'Amen' to your thanksgiving when he does not know what you are saying?" The content of prayer, therefore, is to be revelatory in nature and edifying and instructive to the whole body. Those who lead in corporate prayer should have a high level of maturity in their grasp of the word of God so as to guide the body into the corporate "Amen."

In the preceding passage, Paul virtually identified Spirit-driven prayer with the giving of thanks. The *Westminster Confession* says "Prayer, with thanksgiving, being one special part of religious worship, is by God required of all men."[7] Also, the Colossians passage cited above indicates that watchful prayer involves substantial thanksgiving, and the emphasis on thanksgiving is given again in Philippians 4:6, "In everything by prayer and supplication with thanksgiving let your requests be made known to God." Every request implies a hearty and deeply conscientious sense of dependence on God and a recognition that life and all things have already come to us from him. The Thessalonians received the same admonition, "We urge you brothers . . . pray without ceasing, give thanks in all circumstances" (1 Thessalonians 5:17, 18). While we ask for more as it conforms to his will (1 John 5:14, 15), we are thankful for blessings already received and for the secret providences that sanctify even the severest trials.

Prayer, in fact, rises to a point of serious priority in the public meetings of the church. We find Paul giving the firm instruction to Timothy, "First of all then, I urge that supplications, prayers, intercessions, and thanksgivings be made for all people" (1 Timothy 2:1). Not any level of our social context or any person granted authority should escape the solicitous intercession of the people of God for competence, well-being, and salvation. In the context of the thankful prayers of the church, God grants the atmosphere for a "tranquil and quiet life in all godliness and gravity" (1

---

7 The Second London Confession uses "natural" instead of "religious."

Timothy 2:2 ASV). This is not an illegitimate concern, for Paul repeats it as a word of benediction to the Thessalonian church, "Now may the Lord of peace himself give you peace at all times in every way" (2 Thessalonians 3:17).

The greatest blessing that the body has received, a blessing true of all those gathered for this purpose, is the restoration of the knowledge of God through his truth and his grace. Requests with thanksgiving, therefore, point specifically to gospel proclamation. "At the same time pray for us," Paul continued in Colossians 4, "that God may open to us a door for the word, to declare the mystery of Christ." He wanted to be both clear and bold in this proclamation. Conscious of our indebtedness to faithful proclamation from others, we keep before our minds in worship the necessity of blessings on the means of grace, both for clarity in the message and boldness for the messenger. "How shall they hear without a preacher?" (Romans 10:14). Among the closing words of Paul in Ephesians is his request that, as they are "praying at all times in the Spirit," they remain alert and persevere in "supplications" to be made for him "that words may be given me in opening my mouth boldly to proclaim the mystery of the gospel, for which I am an ambassador in chains, that I may declare it boldly, as I ought to speak" (Ephesians 6:18-20). The church's prayers in corporate worship should be weighted heavily toward clarity and boldness in gospel proclamation. Worship leaders should assure that such prayers regularly appear in the rhythm of worship.

WE PRAY TOGETHER WITH A SPECIFIC CONCERN.

Third, prayer also may emerge in corporate worship in conjunction with the inferences drawn from a guiding text of

Scripture. The power of this should not be underestimated and the warrant for it must be affirmed as a biblical principle. The guiding passage provides the context for praise, thanksgiving, confession and request. For example, suppose the pastor has chosen Psalm 51 as the text for a sermon; in the context the leader chose a theologically thick passage as a guide for worship, such as Romans 5:18-21.

> Therefore, as one trespass led to condemnation for all men, so one act of righteousness leads to justification and life for all men. For as by the one man's disobedience the many were made sinners, so by the one man's obedience the many will be made righteous. Now the law came in to increase the trespass, but where sin increased, grace abounded all the more, so that, as sin reigned in death, grace also might reign through righteousness leading to eternal life through Jesus Christ our Lord.

The worship leader designates that there will be two times of prayer in the worship. The first is a prayer of confession: based on the guiding text, such words as these could be brought before the Lord for the congregation.

> Our gracious God, we come to you in full recognition of the justice of your considering us as under condemnation, for in the most perfect condition of our race, we transgressed your clear and holy command. We confess that not only is such our state as Adam's children, but in our own acts and attitudes we have aggravated it greatly by our personal acts of sin. Even when you have revealed the goodness of your holy Law to us, we have not been arrested in our path of sin, but have sped on with purposeful intent of resisting your holiness. Our continuation in

sin has justly rendered us obnoxious to your wrath and we can plead no goodness of our own, not even a desire for righteousness, or the slightest scintilla of heat toward holiness. We are undone and we find neither in conscience nor in your word any hope of righteousness in ourselves. Our confession is a plea for mercy, for there is one man, even Jesus the Lord through whom we can be accepted as righteous in a way consistent with your justice. We make this confession with an abiding hope in his name, Amen.

The second prayer is one of thanksgiving using the material in the same text.

God and Father of our Lord Jesus Christ, we are indeed amazed at your grace and wisdom. Though our sin is great, your mercy and grace are greater. In your wise and holy plan of redemption you have looked upon our condemned state and set in place a massive reservoir of righteousness in which we can be plunged so as to be covered with it, a sea that is blood red that matches hue for hue our scarlet sins and miraculously dyes us with an indelible white. In spite of our trespasses you have made a just way of forgiveness by one man's obedience. That one act of the one man, that one unbroken act of loving you with all his heart, mind, soul, and strength, and that unbroken sequence of heartfelt obedience, even to the death of the cross now makes many righteous. When your good law increased our hostility and intensified our lawless rebellion, grace yet arrested us. Our hearts overflow with thankfulness. You sent your Son, your beloved Son, to bear our sins in his own body on the tree. How can we not be thankful;

how can any tongue not praise you? Endless, even ever increasing, must be our gratitude and praise. Can anything transcend the gift of eternal life through Jesus Christ our Lord? The gift that is given is great because its giver and procurer is infinitely and wonderfully great. Thanks be to you, now our loving Father, for this inexpressible gift. In the name of our Advocate, even Jesus, we express our thanks, Amen.

The goal of the one who leads corporate worship is to give it faithful expression by the guidance of Scripture in general and to be an exposition of a part of Scripture in particular. Prayer, as an opportunity for praise, as a submission of soul to the purpose and power of God, and as a request for his guidance and glory, may be governed by the guiding text for the day and serve as a means of particular application of revealed truth. The text that guides worship is given exposition in the flow of worship. In turn, it supports the sermonic text and demonstrates the principle of the analogy of faith and the internal consistency of the entire corpus of Scripture.

God graciously redeemed a people for himself, zealous of good works, with a single heart to worship him and know him. He has given them specific instruction concerning how he may be addressed and what requests we may take before him. Not only so, but acknowledging our weakness, our tendency to stray, and thus our need for guidance, like a great Shepherd to his sheep, he has given us a day in which these exercises of unity and supplication may regularly occur.

Chapter Five

READ THE BIBLE, CONFESS ITS MEANING

"The unfolding of your words gives light."
Psalm 119:130

The direct manifestation of Scripture words and propositions guides every gathering for corporate worship. The conformity of each worship element in its particular genre to the authority of the Bible arises from an intentional presentment of express Scripture content. This comes in three manners of presentation: first, the reading of Scripture, second, the recitation of a historic epitome of biblical truth, and, third, the exposition of Scripture by a gifted and called pastor/teacher. These are the means by which God suits us for praise both here and hereafter. This chapter will treat the first two of these and the third, preaching, will be in the next chapter.

READ THE BIBLE

Every time of corporate worship should find its true strength and transforming energy through the reading of Scripture. This happened at the restoration of the Jews from their captivity in Babylon. Ezra the scribe read the book of the Law from morning until midday. Around 50,000 inhabitants gathered for this time of reading and exposition (Nehemiah 7:66, 67; 8:1-3). Ezra and the Levites "read distinctly from the book, in the Law of God; and they gave the sense, and helped them understand the reading" (Ezra 8:8). The people fittingly wept at the revelation of their transgression and unfaithfulness. Nehemiah the governor interrupted their weeping and called them to a time of celebration for they had heard the word of God, had it explained, and had understood it. He said, "This day is holy to our Lord. Do not sorrow, for the joy of the Lord is your strength" (8:10). Many are the effects flowing from the reading of the word, but all of them drive us finally to the presence of joy, and joy issues forth in praise.

The writer of Hebrews, in the final words of his epistle, wrote, "I appeal to you brothers, bear with my word of exhortation, for I have written to you briefly" (Hebrews 13:22). He expected them to have read his entire epistle to the gathered congregation. If he had had confidence in their spiritual maturity, he would have written something longer and more theologically dense (5:11-14)! Even without the advanced course in the superiority of Christ, the letter sets a high standard for what people should be able to glean from the public reading of Scripture. Finally, we will be brought to the place of seeing the end of redemption as Christ himself did—that is, as the "joy set before him" (Hebrews 12:2).

In harmony with that confidence, Paul commanded his most valued messenger, Timothy, "Devote yourself to the public reading of Scripture, to exhortation, to teaching" (1 Timothy 4:13). It seems that the reading came first, to be followed by exhortation and teaching. Paul's letter to Ephesus heightens the importance of reading Scripture within the community of faith and also implies the vanity of looking to other sources for revelatory truth. Paul explained that "the mystery" was made known to him "by revelation as I have *written* briefly." He then proceeded to tell them that "When you *read this*, you can perceive my insight into the mystery of Christ" (Ephesians 3:2, 3). By their public reading of the revelatory truth that had been given to Paul, Paul expected them to see "the unsearchable riches of Christ," "the plan of the mystery hidden for ages in God," and "His eternal purpose that he has realized in Christ Jesus our Lord." All of this is given by revelation, and to be read in Paul's letter "so that through the church the manifold wisdom of God might now be made known to the rulers and authorities in the heavenly places" (Ephesians 3:8-11).

The phrase, "through the church," is to be taken both passively and actively. Passively, the church is acted upon by the determinative grace of God and consists of people of every tongue, and tribe, and people, and nation. This incorporation of such diversity of race, ethnicity, culture, and worldview into a body governed by a commonly embraced truth induces a pleasant astonishment to the rational beings that inhabit the heavenly realm. These are the "things into which angels long to look" (1 Peter 1:12).

Actively, the church shows divine wisdom in two ways. First, as the singular members of this community of called-out ones pursue the divine will and holiness in their lives showing they have been transferred from the kingdom of darkness to the kingdom of his beloved Son, the transforming power and purpose of God is set forth. On the day of visitation, even the lovers of the world who despised God's righteous way will "see your good deeds and glorify God" (Colossians 1:13; 1 Peter 2: 9, 12). Second, as the local bodies of the *ekklesia* gather, their resolution to be governed by a cross-bearing Redeemer, as shown by their unity under the public declaration of the received canon of revealed truth, makes foolish the wisdom of this world and emasculates the supposed virility of its strength (1 Corinthians 1:18-25).

Paul understood his own ministry in accordance with the principle of canon. The revelation that God formerly had given his people was inscripturated. Paul taught that the events of Israel's pilgrimage "were written down for our instruction" (1 Corinthians 10:11). Given that principle, he also knew that the explanation of the new covenant given, written through the apostles, who were "stewards of the mysteries of God" (1 Corinthians 4:1) and were "made competent to be ministers of the new covenant" (2 Corinthians 3:6), had an equal, but clearer and finally fulfilling, canonical status. Their writings and those written down under the careful eye of the apostles would also be canon. Paul wrote with no sense of hesitation or overstatement, "For this we declare to you by a word from the Lord" (1 Thessalonians 4:15), and "these things God revealed to us through the Spirit . . . and we impart this in words not taught by human wisdom but taught by the Spirit" (1 Corinthians 2:10, 13). Also, he reminded the churches of Galatia that the gospel he preached he did not receive from any man but "through a revelation of Jesus Christ." His declaration to Timothy that "All Scripture is given by inspiration of God," included in its context that which he called "my teaching, my aim in life, my faith;" it included the realm of what Timothy had "learned and firmly believed, knowing from whom [he] learned it," meaning the instruction of Paul himself, as well as "the sacred writings." By means of the revelation Paul had received, these writings "are able to make you wise for salvation through faith in Christ Jesus." (2 Timothy 3:10-16) This saving wisdom consists of the Old Testament as now confirmed, clarified, and fulfilled in the work of Christ and the message of the gospel revealed by the Holy Spirit. Peter displayed the same confidence when he identified "the word of the Lord [that] remains forever" with "the good news that was preached to you" (1 Peter 1:25).

As the revelation given through the apostles neared its completion, the need for prophets and tongue-interpreters would decrease accordingly. Their ministry in the churches was to be subservient to the word of the apostles, and thus, could not continue beyond the time of the apostles. To ascertain this in seeking greater order in the church at Corinth, Paul wrote, "If anyone thinks that he is a prophet, or spiritual, he should acknowledge that the things *I am writing* to you are a command of the Lord. If anyone does not recognize this, he is not recognized" (1 Corinthians 14:37, 38). The same confidence incited Paul to tell the Thessalonian Christians, in light of some doctrinal aberrations that had emerged, "If anyone does not obey what we say in this letter, take note of that person, and have nothing to do with him, that he may be ashamed" (2 Thessalonians 3:14). For that reason, his command to the church in Colossae is tantamount to an expectation that their corporate worship would include a heavy dose of reading Scripture: "And when this letter has been read among you, have it also read in the church of the Laodiceans; and see that you also read the letter from Laodicea" (Colossians 4:16).

These letters, under the wise inspiration of the Holy Spirit, served to meet the immediate needs of instruction, correction, exhortation, and encouragement for the churches to whom they were written. At the same time, they constituted and established a final and exclusive authority for the whole community of Christ in perpetuity till he comes again. These lively oracles of the living God need no supplement. Nothing can be added to what the Christ-appointed apostles and Spirit-gifted New Testament prophets (Ephesians 2:20; 3:4, 5) preached and wrote. God gave the New Testament prophetic ministry as a means of speaking revealed truth in the churches while the full corpus of apostolic writing was being produced. The assumption of truth for their revelation was no different from the assumption of truth for the Old Testament prophet. It was precisely the "insight into the mystery of Christ" that was revealed to these prophets.

The New Covenant did not diminish truthful prophecy, but established its clarity and finality. Enough of the confusing and unstable notion that a prophet, speaking under revelatory impulse, might confuse what the Spirit said and unknowingly mix his own unstable opinion with the revelation. The spirituality of Christian worship and the authority under which we proclaim suffers no diminution in the absence of ongoing revelation. Rather, the richness of it is inexhaustible. We have confidence that all we need to know of Christ presently is with us in the written word; the guidance we need for our lives is expressed in divine providence as discerned through increasing conformity of heart to the will of God as expressed in Scripture; and the joy and confidence that the word of God, final, complete, and exclusive, is with us in worship as we glory in the grace and wisdom of his written word.

Peter had the same consciousness about his writing and sent his letters with the expectation that they would be read in the churches. His first letter is addressed, "Peter, an apostle of Jesus Christ, to those who are elect exiles of the dispersion" and ended with this declaration, "By Silvanus, a faithful brother as I regard him, *I have written* briefly to you, exhorting and declaring that *this is the true grace of God. Stand firm in it*" (1 Peter 1:1; 5:12). Again, in 2 Peter 3, Peter wrote, "This is now the second letter that I am writing to you," and made the authority of the apostles parallel to that of the Old Testament prophets: "You should remember the predictions of the holy prophets and the commandment of the Lord and Savior through your apostles." He even commended to them to writings of the Apostle Paul as Scripture, emphasizing that his teaching confirmed and complemented the doctrines of Peter: "Just as our beloved brother Paul also wrote to you according to the wisdom given him, as he does in all his letters, when he speaks in them of these matters" (2 Peter 3:15, 16). Peter worked, that is, wrote, on the premise that the reading of his letter in the church would have an instructive impact and prepare them for both suffering and glory, with a knowledge of God's purpose that gave them support and comfort in the one and joyful anticipation in the other.

John is insistent that his writing carries such spiritual power and propositional clarity that a great number of important issues can be settled if his words and arguments are properly understood. He gave a heads-up early by telling his recipients, "I am writing these things so that our joy may be full" (1 John 1:4). All his doctrinal content is included in the words, "these things," and the final purpose is that our "joy may be full."

Here and now our joy is real and at times virtually dominates our entire outlook. It is never unmixed, however, and so not "full." When joy is full, it harbors no rival beside it to give reservation or pause to the internal sense of it or the external expression. Pressing us toward a clear perception of joy, John says that he is writing that we would love one another because our sins are forgiven for the sake of Jesus' name, we have overcome the evil one, we know him who is from the beginning, we know the Father, and we are strong and the word of God abides in us. (1 John 2:7, 12-14). He writes because we know the truth and we have been taught it with an indelible impression by the anointing of the Spirit (2:21, 26). The tapestry of truth woven into John's words reach their climax when he says, "I write these things to you who believe in the name of the Son of God that you may know that you have eternal life" (1 John 5:13). The assurance of eternal life never comes without the witness of the written word.

The finality of the written word is illustrated in the revelation given to John on Patmos. On two occasions, the apostle John was so overwhelmed with the appearance of an angel that he bowed in worship. In Revelation 19:10, the angel responded, "You must not do that. I am a fellow servant with you and your brothers who hold to the testimony of Jesus. Worship God." John then commented, "For the testimony of Jesus is the spirit of prophecy." In 22:8 the angel responded similarly, "You must not do that! I am a fellow servant with you and your brothers the prophets, and with those who keep the words of this book. Worship God." The prophets to whom the angel referred were the New Testament prophets, those who (verse 10) "held the testimony of Jesus" in the churches until the completion of this testimony. That completion was to occur at the end of the next 13 verses of Revelation 22. The angel, the apostle, and the Lord Jesus complete the prophetic word: "I, Jesus have sent my angel to testify to you about these things for the churches. I am the root and the descendant of David, the bright morning star." The Spirit and the Bride (the church) entreat all who will hear this word to take freely and abundantly of the water of eternal life. Then a stern warning is given to any who "hears the words of the prophecy of this book" that he is not to add to them at the risk of receiving the plagues described in the book. Nor is any to take from "the words of the book of this prophecy" under the threat of a similar consequence (Revelation 22:18, 19). By extension this must apply to the entire New Testament as the work of the apostles and prophets. None could make the argument, "One may not subtract from or add to the Apocalypse, but one can do so to Matthew, Mark, Luke, John, Romans, etc." Nor can one credibly suggest that to add to the New Testament canon, or detract from it, does not violate the warning at the end of Revelation. John as the last living apostle sees the revelation he is given coming to an end. The words ordained of God through the apostles and prophets reached their point of culmination and absolute sufficiency for the life of the Christian and the church until the Lord returns. That Jesus himself gave this word of finality through the pen of John is ascertained in the words of verse 20, "He who testifies to these things says, 'Surely I am coming soon.' Amen. Come, Lord Jesus!" The last of the apostles dies, the prophetic utterance in the churches resolves fully into Scripture, and angels do their work without observation.

CONCENTRATED SCRIPTURE TRUTH

As an aid in the admonition to teach one another from the word of Christ dwelling in us, congregational worship should employ historic confessions of faith. We will give more space to this later, but, in this context, we give one illustration of its value. This practice is a normal part of many Christian liturgies. Roman Catholics, Greek Orthodox, Anglicans, Presbyterians, and Methodists regularly recite together the Apostles' Creed and at times the Nicene Creed as expanded in Constantinople in 381. Sometimes congregations having Dutch Reformed roots will recite elements of the *Heidelberg Catechism*. These practices honor biblical truth, give voice to common Christian belief, provide opportunity for sound doctrinal instruction, and tie the congregation to the "faith once for all delivered to the saints."

For example, say the minister selects Romans 7:7-12 as the text for the sermon.

> *What then shall we say?*
> *That the law is sin? By no means!*
> *Yet if it had not been for the law,*
> *I would not have known sin.*
> *For I would not have known what it is to covet if the law had not said, "You shall not covet."*
> *But sin, seizing an opportunity through the commandment, produced in me all kinds of covetousness.*
> *For apart from the law, sin lies dead.*
> *I was once alive apart from the law, but when the commandment came, sin came alive and I died.*
> *The very commandment that promised life proved to be death to me.*
> *For sin, seizing an opportunity through the commandment deceived me and through it killed me.*
> *So the law is holy,*
> *and the commandment is holy and righteous and good.*

The final section, verses 169-176, of Psalm 119 is selected as the supportive text to guide worship. That section emphasizes the desirability, the delightfulness, and the rightness of God's law, but at the same time the psalmist expresses longing for salvation, confesses having gone astray, and requests for life in his soul that he might live in praise to God. It carries within it the use of the law to drive one to a redeemer and to prompt the true worshiper to holiness and praise.

> Let my cry come before you, O Lord;
> Give me understanding according to your word.
> Let my plea come before you;
> Deliver me according to your word,
> My lips will pour forth praise,
> For you teach me your statutes.
> My tongue will sing of your word
> For all your commandments are right.
> Let your hand be ready to help me,
> For I have chosen your precepts.
> I long for your salvation, O Lord,
> And your law is my delight.
> Let my soul live and praise you,
> And let your rules help me.
> I have gone astray like a lost sheep;
> Seek your servant,
> For I do not forget your commandments.

This guiding text offers opportunities for prayer, praise, conviction and confession of sin, expressions of dependence, affirmation of the truth of the word of God, and in general contributes to the biblical doctrine of law and gospel when rightly discerned. One element that can contribute to coherence of the understanding and affirmation of divine truth would be a congregational recitation, or a responsive reading built on an excellent confessional article on law and gospel. *The Westminster Confession*, the *Second London Confession*, and the *Savoy Declaration* contain such a statement that could easily be arranged as a responsive reading. This is taken from the *Second London Confession* with some updating of language and slight editorial changes for conciseness and clarification.

Leader:

> Although true believers are not under the law as a covenant of works, to be justified or condemned by it, yet it is of great use to them as well as to others, in that as a rule of life, it informs them of the will of God and their duty, so they may walk according to its precepts.

Congregation:

> It also unveils the sinful pollutions of their natures, hearts, and lives, so that they may examine themselves by it, and may thus come to further conviction of, humiliation for, and hatred against, sin.

Leader:

> These operations of the Law on the heart give a clearer sight of the need they have of Christ and the perfection of his obedience;

Congregation:

> It is likewise of use to the regenerate to restrain their corruptions, in that it forbids sin; its threatenings show what even their sins deserve, and what afflictions in this life they may expect for them, although freed from the curse and, thus, the punitive rigor of its threats.

Leader:

> The promises of it likewise show them God's approval of obedience, and what blessings they may expect upon the performance of it, though not as due to them by the law as a covenant of works, but as blessings of grace.

Congregation:

> So man's doing good and refraining from evil, because the law encourages to the one and deters from the other, does not contradict the truth, but rather confirms it, that we are not under law but under grace, and that those who live by the Spirit, also will walk by the Spirit.

A guiding text for worship, consonant with the text for preaching, opens avenues for every biblically mandated aspect of worship while giving coherence to the family of thoughts connected with it. The guiding text secures the minds of the worship participants for the revealed truth involved. Reading the Bible and drawing attention to concise statements of its teaching can be vital elements of teaching ourselves to praise God in Spirit and truth.

THE FELLOWSHIP OF KINDRED MIND

In the state of eternal life our joy is full and our knowledge of God—his purpose and his glory—enters a new and unending expansiveness. Fullness of joy thrives in the presence of God in heaven. "Joy inexpressible and full of glory" (1 Peter 1:8) immediately invades every space created by our ever-expanding capacities for unalloyed spiritual pleasure in the unfiltered beauty and satisfaction of the presence of

God. Till then, we prepare ourselves for it. Our experience of it is real, built on those momentary expansions of spirit in which we sense something of wonder of the presence of a graciously redeeming God. Even those high times, however, are miniscule compared to its full display in eternity.

The place in which it most resembles heaven is in the meeting of the community where God's truths are spoken, sung, and heard with united hearts. Scripture-guided worship, including the intentional focus on the text of Scripture and its exposition through a variety of means is not merely pragmatically helpful in constructing an order of worship, but what the apostles expected when they wrote the words of revelation.

Chapter Six

Repentance and Remission of Sins Should Be Preached in His Name

"The preaching with which I have been entrusted, . . . teach what accords with sound doctrine. . . . in your teaching show integrity. . . . I want you to insist on these things."
Titus 1:3; 2:1, 7; 3:8

Unadorned Proclamation

We are introduced to the public ministry of Jesus with the words, "In those days John the Baptist came preaching in the wilderness of Judea." Soon Jesus came to align his ministry with the proclamation and call to repentance that came from John's lips: "Then Jesus came from Galilee to the Jordan to John, to be baptized by him" (Matthew 3:1, 13). In this act of submission, Jesus affirmed that John the Baptist was a true prophet, that his message was the true message, and that his manner of communication was the designated way of distributing the truth.

Also, Jesus identified himself with the humanity that he came to save by entering into the implications of righteousness invested in the message of immersion on the basis of repentance: "Thus it is fitting for us to fulfill all righteousness." He was qualified to be a covenant head of sinners and had identified with them both in his incarnation and now in the bath of cleansing, a foretelling of the baptism with which he would close his earthly work for sinners (Mark 10:38; Hebrews 2:17, 18). His personal perfection in the context of both baptisms was verified from heaven with the words, "This is my beloved Son, with whom I am well pleased" (Matthew 3:17; 17:5).

After Jesus had come through the first Spiritually designated time of severe testing (Matthew 4:1; Mark 1:12; Luke 4:1; 1 Timothy 3:16), he soon heard that John the Baptist had been arrested. Immediately, he aligned his life with fulfilling John's announcement that one mightier and infinitely more worthy than he, one who was the very lamb of God (Matthew 3:1; Luke 3:14; John 1:27, 36) stood in their midst. Jesus, therefore, "began to preach" (Matthew 4:17). Beginning as a lone itinerant, he soon called followers and began teaching crowds in natural settings and in the formal setting of the synagogue (Matthew 4:18; 5:1, 2; Luke 4:16-19). His preaching arose from biblical authority (Matthew 5:17, 18; 22:29; Luke 4:17-22), indicated original authority (Matthew 5:43-48; 7:29), was simple in its assertions (7:12), uncompromising in its content (Matthew 23:13-15), and often infuriating in its outcome (Luke 4:24-29).

The preaching of John the Baptist and Jesus was unadorned, unaccompanied by any other accoutrements of worship. This indicates that the heart of worship, the manner in which God restores us to the high calling of praise, always is the proclamation of the word. Those activities of the congregation that surround the context of preaching must not detract from it but, as it were, become a part of it. All that God has mandated as elemental to worship moves toward that end; leaders must value this stewardship.

The Burden

When John Broadus considered the magnitude of all that God invested in preaching, he lamented, "Oh it is so hard to preach as one ought to do! I long for the opportunity, yet do not rise to meet it with whole-souled earnestness and living faith, and afterwards I feel sad and ashamed."[1] Everyone who has preached has felt that same sense of shortcoming. Scripture—a revelation captured in words by inspiration, thus of infallible authority, and thus of inerrant propositions when accurately deduced from the text—provides the content of the message. Through preaching, so through preachers, this faith-generating truth is set before the hearts through the ears of saints and sinners, an aroma of death to the one and of life to the other. This reality caused Broadus again to reflect, "Did not feel as much tenderness as the subject ought to inspire. Oh, that I could myself be deeply moved by the preciousness of religion and the perilous condition of those who neglect it!"[2] If one has not felt the weight of this calling so as to say with Paul, "Who is sufficient for these things" (2 Corinthians 2:16), then he is not ready to enjoy the freedom that comes in saying, "Not that we are sufficient of ourselves to think of anything as being from ourselves, but our sufficiency is from God" (2 Corinthians 3:5).

Paul did not do as many did even so early in the history of the church. He did not peddle the word of God, nor did

---

1 A. T. Robertson, *Life and Letters of John A. Broadus* (Philadelphia: American Baptist Publication Society, 1909), 200.
2 Robertson, 137.

he use "flattering words" as a cloak for covetousness, nor did he handle the word of God craftily or deceitfully (2 Corinthians 1:17; 1 Thessalonians 2:5; 2 Corinthians 4:2). Instead, with a clear view of what word he spoke and what was at stake for the hearer, he spoke sincerely "in the sight of God in Christ . . . to be well-pleasing to him" with the intent of persuading those who heard him that his message was true. He had been "approved by God to be entrusted with the gospel" and under the gravity of that calling, he spoke, "not as pleasing men, but God who tests our hearts" (2 Corinthians 2:17; 5:11; 1 Thessalonians 2:4). Truth was constantly in his mind, upon his heart, and on his lips. Only in the "manifestation of the truth" would he want to be commended to any listener; he knew his message was "in truth, the word of God" (2 Corinthians 4:2; 1 Thessalonians 2:13). Nevertheless, his sincerity and transparent devotion to God and revealed truth would accomplish no good unless it were "written by the Spirit of the living God on tablets of the heart." The message must not come "in word only" but with a special convincing and converting efficacy of the Holy Spirit. (2 Corinthians 4:3; 1 Thessalonians 1:4, 5).

Worship and evangelism come by Spirit and truth. The part of this spiritual transaction that is most clearly resident within our personal stewardship is the ministry of the word. God will send his Spirit either to harden or to call by grace, but, in either case, the task given us is to highlight the truth. Every gathering for worship is a God-ordained event in which his people, led by God-fitted ministers of truth, take advantage of every moment for making the message clear and plain. The purpose of this time of assembly is given the greatest opportunity for spiritual success when the entire time moves toward the understanding of the sermon text for the day. A Scripture-guided approach to worship honors the proclamation of God's word by streamlining the entire worship toward its exposition.

Proclamation

The preaching that leads to justification and the preaching that leads to sanctification occur in the same moment in corporate worship. A biblical text, set within its relevant immediate and larger canonical context, to which exposition is given is full of God glorifying, soul-transforming power and truth. The unjustified are confronted with their guilt and the promise of life in Christ, and the justified see more clearly the duty, glory, and path of holiness.

The entire worship experience that resolves into such proclamation forms the channel of truth through which the preached word will flow. In reality, the exercise of worship that surrounds proclamation is a part of the proclamation itself. It focuses the heart on content, ideas, attitudes, and coherence of biblical truth out of which the preached word finds a receptive ear. The whole body of worship establishes a sense of profound relevance for the text under consideration in the sermon.

That all worship should serve to establish attention on the preaching can hardly be challenged. Paul summarized both content and method of making known the gospel when he stated, "It pleased God through the folly of what we preach to save those who believe." The "what" part refers to Christ and him crucified as the wisdom and power of God. The "we preach" part refers to the method of its dispensing. Both of these ideas are contained in one word—*kerugmatos*—in the original language. The message delivered and the manner of its delivery are bound up with each other.

As Paul continued, "We preach (same root word) Christ crucified." Later he pointed to the non-negotiable character of his message by calling it "the testimony of God" and reinforced its manner by saying that this testimony given by God himself is what he "proclaimed" (different word that means to *announce with power*). Further he explained, in emphasizing his confidence in the words of divine revelation, that "my word and my preaching" (back to the original word) were not in the theoretically persuasive words of wisdom, such as would be endorsed by the rhetoricians of Corinth, but, on the contrary, he stuck with the message dependent on the power of the Spirit. In doing this, Paul could say with confidence that their resultant profession of belief did not rest on the wisdom of man but on the power of God (1 Corinthians 1:21-2:5).

It was not a propensity to megalomania, but of careful adherence to his office as an apostle, that drove Paul to tell Timothy to charge "certain persons not to teach any different doctrine"—that is, different from that which Paul delivered to Timothy. He was to "guard the deposit entrusted" to him. In accord with the truth revealed to Paul and delivered as a deposit to Timothy, he was to function in his role as a pastor/teacher. "Teach and urge these things" Paul admonished. "If anyone teaches a different doctrine and does not agree with the sound words of our Lord Jesus Christ and the teaching that accords with godliness, he is puffed up with conceit and understands nothing" (1 Timothy 1:3; 6:2, 3, 20). This is a severe judgment on one who seeks to find something more effective, more appealing, more with-it, than the "faith once for all delivered to the saints" (Jude 3).

Not only is the teaching to "agree with the sound words" given by and about our Lord Jesus Christ, but all aspects of worship should point to that same agreement. If it can be shown that within the biblical corpus there is a profound agreement of Scripture with Scripture, that one portion affirms another, and at times clarifies and expands it, then the weightiness of worship in being biblically-driven sticks to the conscience in a profound way. A Scripture-driven order of worship gives existential demonstration to the necessity of our agreement with the text and reinforces the authority of the text. If the Bible agrees with the Bible, who are we to depart from it for another avenue to truth and godliness?

Neither Paul nor Timothy controlled the medium or the content of communication. Preaching, proclamation, and teaching in an urgent manner was the method. The revelatory deposit set forth in a "pattern of sound words," an organized manner of presentation governed by Scripture, defined the preaching ministry (2 Timothy 1:13). The preacher has no option but to pursue this; the church has no option but to make it the driving element of corporate worship. Paul knew that both his preaching and his message did not arise from his will but as stewardship placed upon him so that he could say clearly, "Woe to me if I do not preach the gospel" (1 Corinthians 9:16).

Alexander MacLaren (1826-1910), preacher at Union Chapel in Manchester, England, used Jonah's preaching to the Ninevites to give these observations on the serious call of the preacher.

> The word rendered "preach" is instructive. It means "to cry" and suggests the manner benefitting those who bear God's message. They should sound it out loudly, plainly, urgently, with earnestness and marks of emotion in their voices. Languid whispers will not wake sleepers. Unless the messenger is manifestly in earnest, the message will fall flat. Not with bated

breath, as if ashamed of it; nor with hesitation, as if not quite sure of it; nor with coldness, as if it were of little urgency,—is God's Word to be pealed in men's ears. The preacher is a crier. The substance of his message, too, is set forth. 'The preaching which I bid thee'—not his own imaginations, nor any fine things of his own spinning. Suppose Jonah had entertained the Ninevites with dissertations on the evidence of his prophetic authority, or submitted for their consideration a few thoughts tending to show the agreement of his message with their current opinions in religion, or an argument for the existence of a retributive Governor of the world, he would not have shaken the city. The less the Prophet shows himself, the stronger his influence. The more simply he repeats the stern, plain, short message, the more likely it is to impress. God's word, faithfully set forth, will prove itself. The preacher or teacher of this day has substantially the same charge as Jonah had; and the more he suppresses himself, and becomes but a voice through which God speaks, the better for himself, his hearers, and his work."[3]

Woe to us, a sickness unto death it will be to us, insipidity in any attempt to worship God should we grow weary of the proclamation of the cross. It is not a scheme to be minimized at any time or in any place where the purpose is the church's worship of the triune God. Paul insisted that Timothy "Preach the word; be ready in season and out of season; reprove, rebuke, and exhort, with complete patience and teaching" (2 Timothy 4:2).

---

3 Alexander MacLaren, *MacLaren's Exposition of Holy Scripture*, (Grand Rapids: William B. Eerdman's, 1959) 4:190-91..

THE EXAMPLE OF CHARLES SPURGEON

Charles Spurgeon adhered to this idea of internal agreement among the elements of worship. Though his service was much more plain than modern day worship, though he eschewed instruments and choirs and special music in corporate worship on the Lord's day, he nevertheless organized the entire service around the exposition of a governing passage of Scripture. For example, on April 25, 1875, Spurgeon preached a sermon entitled "The Sure Triumph of the Crucified One." The text for the sermon was Isaiah 52:13-15 (KJV).[4]

> [13] *Behold, my servant shall deal prudently,*
> *he shall be exalted and extolled, and be very high.*
> [14] *As many were astonied at thee;*
> *his visage was so marred more than any man,*
> *and his form more than the sons of men:*
> [15] *So shall he sprinkle many nations;*
> *the kings shall shut their mouths at him:*
> *for that which had not been told them shall they see;*
> *and that which they had not heard shall they consider.*

At an appointed place in the service, Spurgeon read the entire chapter of Isaiah 53. This was his regular practice, to give an extended reading of a passage which contained his text or that was closely related to his text and give brief expository remarks on it. Because of its familiarity, he made few comments but inserted one after verse 9—And he made his grave with the wicked, and with the rich in his death; because he hath done no violence, neither was any deceit in his mouth.

---

4 Charles Spurgeon, *The Metropolitan Tabernacle Pulpit* (Pasadena, Tx: Pilgrim Publications, 1971), 21:241-252.

Spurgeon noted, "A strange reason for making his grave with the wicked, and yet remember if it had not been that he had done no violence, he would not have been fit to be a substitute for sinners, and so he was numbered with transgressors so as to redeem men." After verse 12, he commented,

> How clearly you have before you here our blessed Redeemer, and how strong are the expressions used by Isaiah to set forth his substitution. If he did intend to teach us the doctrine that Christ suffered in the place and stead of his people, he could not have used more expressive words; and if he did not intend to teach us that truth, it is marvelous that he should have adopted a phraseology so likely to mislead. Yes, we believe and hold it fast, that Christ did take the sins of his people verily and truly upon himself, and did in proper person make a complete expiation for the guilt of all his chosen, and in this we find our hearts' best confidence.[5]

The emphasis of the message was, that though from a human standpoint, many found nothing attractive in Jesus as the marred victim of human hate and punishment, yet he shall be exalted and extolled by the preaching of the word and the regenerating power of the Holy Spirit so that he gains all and loses nothing by such disfigurement. "Let us brace ourselves up this morning," he encouraged, "with the delightful prospect of the predestinated triumph of the kingdom of our Lord and of his Christ."

Again, as a summary of another part of his argument, Spurgeon affirmed, "The decrees of God will be

---

5 Charles Spurgeon, "Commentary on Isaiah 53," Spurgeon's Verse Expositions of the Bible, accessed April 19, 2021, https://www.studylight.org/commentaries/eng/spe/isaiah-53.html.

accomplished; his eternal purposes will be fulfilled. . . . The blood of Jesus Christ will not miss of its foreseen result in reference to any individual under heaven, and no end that was designed in the eternal plan of redemption shall be left unaccomplished." Though the marring of Jesus makes some stumble, the marring itself is that which gives hope to sinners in need of redemption and constitutes the beauty of the savior in the day of his power. "Jesus, thou marred One, thy cross, instead of being a stumbling-block to us, is the glory of our faith."

Though kings do not shut their mouths in his presence now, but rather open them against him, another time is coming. "We look for this, and come it will. O thorn-crowned King of Calvary, kings shall be thy courtiers yet!" Again, Spurgeon assured his auditory that the text "claims for Jesus Christ that the influence of his grace and the power of his work shall be extended over many nations, and shall have power not over the common people only, but over their leaders and rulers."

Work, hard labor in the gospel, clear and unfaltering preaching all are commended as ways in which Jesus' gospel will succeed. Jesus never will forsake the preaching of his word, the word of the cross, as the instrument of victory. "I believe," Spurgeon announced, "that this battle is to be fought out on the line upon which it began. It pleases God by the foolishness of preaching to save them that believe." On this God-ordained manner and matter, "The success of the gospel is in no jeopardy whatever. Jesus must reign till he hath put all enemies under his feet." Spurgeon closed his message with an apostrophe to enemy and friend alike.

> Stand back, devils! When God's bare arm comes into the fight, you will all run like dogs, for you know your Master. Stand back, heresies and schisms, evils

and delusions; you will all disappear, for the Christ of God is mightier than you. Oh, believe it. Do not be downhearted and dispirited, do not run to new schemes and fancies and interpretations of prophecy. Go and preach Jesus Christ unto all the nations. Go and spread abroad the Saviour's blessed name, for he is the world's only hope. The cross is the banner of our victory. God help us to look to it ourselves, and then to hold it up before the eyes of others, till our Lord shall come upon his throne. Amen.

The hymns interspersed through the service all supported the theme of the reading exposition and the main emphases of the sermon.[6] They sang,

> *Jesus shall reign where'er the sun does*
> *his successive journeys run;*
>
> *His Kingdom spread from shore to shore, till*
> *moons shall wax and wane no more.*
>
> *For him shall endless prayers be made,*
> *and praises throng to crown his head;*
>
> *His name like sweet perfume shall rise*
> *with every morning sacrifice.*

Continuing the exegetical theme of the reign of the marred and crucified one, they sang also,

> *Crown him with many crowns,*
> *the lamb upon His throne;*
>
> *Hark how the heavenly anthem*
> *drowns all music but its own.*

---

6 C. H. Spurgeon, comp. *Our Own Hymnbook* (London: Passmore and Alabaster, 1878), nos. 72, 418, 352.

> *Awake my soul, and sing*
> *of Him who died for thee;*
> *And hail Him as the matchless king*
> *through all eternity.*
>
> *Crown him the Lord of Love;*
> *behold His hands and side;*
>
> *Rich wounds, yet visible above*
> *in beauty glorified.*

Those themes plus others that flowed within Spurgeon's development of the theme were caught in a hymn by Michael Bruce.

> *Behold the mountain of the Lord in latter days shall rise*
> *on mountain-tops, above the hills,*
> *and draw the wondering eyes.*
>
> *To this the joyful nations round, all*
> *tribes and tongues shall flow;*
> *Up to the hill of God, they'll say, and to his house we'll go.*
>
> *The beam that shines from Zion*
> *hill shall lighten every land;*
>
> *the King that reigns in Salem's towers*
> *shall all the world command.*

The Prince of Preachers, the purveyor of great simplicity in worship, found his theme in a guiding text and developed it in exposition, prayer, singing, and sermon.

Chapter Seven

THE CONGREGATION SINGS

"They shall sing aloud of your righteousness."
Psalm 145:7

"I will sing of the steadfast love of the Lord forever."
Psalm 89:1

MUSIC EVOKES TRANSCENDENT THEMES FROM IMPASSIONED HEARTS

A singularly effective manner of communicating the truth of divine revelation in corporate worship is community testimony and instruction through song. As an outflow of spiritual fullness, and from the melody in the heart, we are to "speak to one another in psalms, hymns, and spiritual songs." From the rich indwelling of the word of Christ, and from grace in the heart, we are given to "teaching and admonishing one another in psalms, hymns, and spiritual songs." (Ephesians 5:19; Colossians 3:16). This engagement of mind, emotion, articulation, and affection establishes a channel through which the river of spiritual instruction from the word of God may flow. David found the celebration of the power and redeeming grace of God a constant source of singing praise (Psalm 59:16, 17).

> *But I will sing of Your power;*
> *Yes, I will sing aloud of Your mercy*
> *In the morning;*
> *For you have been my defense*
> *And refuge in the day of my trouble.*
> *To You, O my strength, I will sing praises;*
> *For God is my defense,*
> *My God of mercy.*

Sung texts that reinforce the *content* of a guiding Scripture also prompt the hidden cisterns of *emotional* reserve to flow into a collective stream of uniform verbal and vocal expression. Moods may be captured in musical modes; both lamentation and joy may be given community expression by ascending and descending lines of melody. Harmony can enchant the soul with an unanswerable wonder at the beauty that surrounds us. The mathematical arrangement of sound waves transferred from vibrating vocal cords to vibrating air waves by divine design gives a faint prospect of the transcendence of inexhaustible harmony in a united manifestation of beauty that constitutes God himself. Jonathan Edwards contemplated that "Singing is amiable, because of the proportion that is perceived in it; singing in divine worship is beautiful and useful, because it expresses and promotes the harmonious exercise of mind."[7]

Heaven continues this sense of beauty and perfection in an ever-increasing way. Both melody and harmony become so entwined in our perceptions that the increasing holiness in heaven, the increasing fellowship between the saints, and that of the saints with the triune God compose one unending song of exquisite beauty the production of which we are entirely incapable here (Revelation 5:8-14). Verse 9 uses the

---

7 Jonathan Edwards, Yale *Works*. 13:303.

phrase, "And they sang a new song, saying," followed by the words of the song. That juxtaposition of words, "sang . . . , saying" combined with the language of 15:3, "They sing the song of Moses . . . saying" could indicate that all of these verses said in chorus are sung. See the texts of 4:8, 11; 5:9, 10, 12, 13; 7:12; 11:17, 18; 15:3, 4; 19:6, 7. The realities of creation, providence, redemption, judgment, and final consummation provide the material for the songs. Everything that God has done is of such excellent character that his people may sing about all of it. God has not given the gift of music and its undeniable connection with expressive emotion analogous to the incorruptible melody and harmony of heaven to be frittered away on garbage, in celebration of idolatrous worldly trivialities. He meant it to be used to worship him in Spirit and in truth.

Music a Biblical Vehicle for Truth

It seems that "the music of the spheres" was discovered by Jubal who found ways to capture a variety of melodic and harmonic sounds endearing to the soul through the ear by his development of the harp and flute (Genesis 4:21). The celebration and instructive capacities of Moses gave precedent to the content and mood of worship through song. He established the exalted purpose of drawing the people to an acknowledgement of God's intervention in human affairs for the manifestation of his glory and the fitting response of his people (Exodus 15:1-3). "Then Moses and the people of Israel sang this song to the Lord, saying,

> *I will sing to the Lord,*
> *For he has triumphed gloriously;*
> *The horse and his rider*
> *He had thrown into the sea.*

> *The Lord is my strength and my song,*
> *And he has become my salvation;*
> *This is my God, and I will exalt him.*
> *The Lord is a man of war;*
> *The Lord is his name.*

As the ministry of Moses came to a close, again he set forth the words of a song that celebrated the faithful goodness of God and gave poetic permanence to human shame by composing verse about the perverse unfaithfulness of the people (Deuteronomy 32:1-47). He began,

> *Give ear O heavens, and I will speak,*
> *And let earth hear the words of my mouth.*
> *May my teaching drop as the rain,*
> *My speech as the dew,*
> *Like gentle rain upon the tender grass,*
> *And like showers upon the herb.*
> *For I will proclaim the name of the Lord;*
> *Ascribe greatness to our God!*
> *The Rock, his work is perfect, for all his ways are justice.*
> *A God of faithfulness and without iniquity.*

Moses then supplied plenty of verses describing the sin, corruption, unmindfulness, and twistedness of the people.

> *But Jeshuran grew fat and kicked;*
> *You grew fat, you grew thick, you are obese!*
> *Then he forsook God who made him,*
> *And scornfully esteemed the Rock of his salvation.*
> *They provoked him to jealousy*
> *With foreign gods;*
> *With abominations*
> *They provoked Him to anger.*

This they were also to acknowledge as the dark background for the manifestation of divine intervention: "For the Lord will vindicate his people and have compassion on his servants, when he sees that their power is gone and there is none remaining, bond or free" (Deuteronomy 32:36). Were their senseless deportment reduced to the verse of a modern hymn, it might read in the words of Horatius Bonar,

> "Ah, mine iniquity, crimson hath been.
> Infinite, infinite, sin upon sin.
> Sin of not loving Thee,
> sin of not trusting Thee—infinite sin."[8] (?

The same necessity of having confession of sin as an element of what we sing modeled under the inspired Moses and faithfully embraced by writers of hymns we find in Phillip Doddridge:

> Ungrateful sinners,
> Whence this scorn of long-extended grace?
> And whence this madness
> That insults the Almighty to His face?
> Is it because his patience waits,
> And pitying bowels move,
> You multiply audacious crimes,
> And spurn His richest love?[9]

But we do not leave our voices' proclamation of sin as an unresolved absolute. It is a matter of singing because it is in the context of the infinite glory of a forgiving God. Psalm 32 provides instruction centered on the clear hope of forgiveness. It is the first of the Psalms called a *Maschil*, a word that denotes "instruction." That is abundantly appropriate for this Psalm and for its usefulness in corporate worship. It tells how God, through the experience of sin and confession, instructed

---

8 Horatius Bonar, "No, Not Despairingly," *The Baptist Hymnal* (Nashville: Convention Press, 1991), hymn # 270.

9 Philip Doddridge, "Treasuring Up Wrath by Despising Mercy," in *Hymns of Philip Doddridge*, comp and ed Graham Ashworth (Grand Rapids: Soli Deo Gloria Publications, 2010) 106, hymn # 258.,

David; then, in turn, the psalmist enters into the mode of instructing those who read and sing it. The content of the instruction bears heavily on the entire message of the Bible, extending back to Genesis 3:15, 21 and continuing through Paul's argument in Romans, Galatians, and Philippians. It becomes a major source for expanding the biblical revelation of God's wisdom and grace in justification. The instruction in this psalm is a treasure of truths surrounding that doctrine "by which the church stands or falls," the doctrine of justification by faith, more fully expanded in other places throughout Scripture. "How blessed is he whose transgression is forgiven, whose sin is covered! How blessed is the man to whom the Lord does not impute iniquity" (Psalm 32:1, 2).

Both the spirit and the instruction are caught well in the words that the Presbyterian Samuel Davies prompts us to sing, "Who is a pard'ning God like Thee, and who has grace so rich and free."[10] The Baptist Benjamin Beddome found confession of sin to be a fit subject for singing as a prelude for grateful praise as he incorporates another idea in the psalm, "in whose spirit there is no deceit" (Psalm 32:2b).

> *Astonish'd and distress'd,*
> *I turn mine eyes within:*
> *My heart with loads of guilt oppress'd*
> *The seat of every sin.*
> *What crowds of evil thoughts,*
> *What vile affections there!*
> *Envy and pride, deceit and guile,*
> *Distrust and slavish fear.*
> *Almighty King of Saints,*
> *These tyrant lusts subdue;*

---

10 Samuel Davies, "Great God of Wonders," in *Spurgeon's Own Hymnbook* comp. C. H. Spugeon, ed. Chris Fenner & Matt Boswell (Ross-shire, Scotland: Christian Focus, 2019) Hymn # 202.

> *Drive the old serpent from his seat,*
> *And all my powers renew.*
> *This done, my cheerful voice*
> *Shall loud hosannas raise;*
> *My soul shall glow with gratitude,*
> *My lips proclaim Thy praise.*[11]

The intrinsic goodness of God, the perverse rebellion and consequent need of man, and the multifaceted grace of God's redeeming purpose provide the source for sung worship. Charles Spurgeon opted for a broad manifestation of content in *Our Own Hymnbook*. "If any object," Spurgeon reasoned, "that some of the hymns are penitential or doctrinal, and therefore unfit to be sung, we reply that we find examples of such in the Book of Psalms which we have made our model in compiling our work." He determined not to "fall in with modern scruples" but rest content with "ancient precedents."[12]

All of the people of God, transformed by Jesus' dying love, give vent to the internal pressure of their desire both to confess sin and unworthiness and to praise redeeming grace through the managed arrangement of corporate song. The redemption of the life involves the redemption of the lips. The gratitude of the heart, in well-conceived corporate worship, flows through words fired into truthful expression by faithful combination of tune and text that launches the doctrines of the Bible into the very space of the praising church.

---

11 Benjamin Beddome, "Astonished and Distressed" in *Spurgeon's Own Hymnbook, Hymn # 644*.
12 Charles Spurgeon, *Our Own Hymnbook* (London: Passmore & Alabaster, 1878 (originally published 1866).

HISTORICAL RENEWAL OF CORPORATE PRAISE

Singing in corporate worship was rescued from its medieval captivity to called professionals, the clergy, and given back to the people, the laity, in the Reformation. Martin Luther (1483-1546) lamented the professionalization of singing that had driven song to be in service of "a hope for gain, or a fear of punishment, injury, and shame." Nothing was done with the intent "to further the knowledge of the Word of God." The words were in Latin and the styles were largely mystical and ethereal. They did not lack beauty, a sense of holy austerity, and transcendence, but they largely prohibited participation by common people. Luther wanted music in the service of theology to be a mode of expression for the people and a teacher of basic gospel truth. The psalms of Scripture were not to be mumbled in an incomprehensible murmur as the monks and priests did. He believed that psalms and hymns as mentioned in Colossians 3:16 were texts provided in Scripture itself such as the psalms of David and others and the hymn of Moses, Deborah, Habakkuk, and the Magnificat. Spiritual songs are "those not written in the Scriptures but of daily origin with men." Luther gave his own hand to such songs, because, for Luther, music gave charm and was a valid outlet for the beauty of poetry. He saw Paul's desire as having "the Word of God to dwell among Christians generally, and richly to be spoken, sung and meditated upon everywhere; and that understandingly and productive of spiritual fruit, the Word being universally prized." This kind of "heartfelt praise and thanks" was to dwell among them, "not merely lodge as a guest for a night or two, but abide with you forever."[13]

---

13 Martin Luther, *Sermons* 7 vols. (Grand Rapids: Baker Book House, 2000), 4:90. 91.

John Calvin (1509-1564) heard German hymns and psalms sung at Strasbourg. This striking experience within its theological and liturgical context prompted him to give verse to psalms and arrange for interesting, even lively, ("Geneva Jigs" according to Queen Elizabeth) tunes to give congregations pleasant participation in the ministry of the word. His commentary on Colossians 3:16 pointed to singing as an expression of doctrine—the word of Christ dwelling in us—wisely applied as a spur to virtue. All of our words should promote edification so that "even those which serve cheerfulness may not be pointless." When truth is expressed in the mirth of music, Christian joy and character enlarge. He explained, "It becomes you to sing hymns and songs that sound forth God's praise." The categories included "all kinds of songs." The psalms were to be sung with the accompaniment of musical instruments, hymns were songs of praise, "whether it be sung simply with the voice or otherwise," and a spiritual song employs praises but also "exhortations and other matters." While the Anabaptists believed that the phrase "in your hearts" meant not audibly but only by personal meditation, Calvin said that Paul did not mean inward singing only. Instead, "this relates to feeling; for as we ought to stir up others, so also we ought to sing from the heart, that there may not be merely an outward sound with the mouth." True spiritual feeling, that is, a deeply sensed grateful dependence on grace, gives rise to rightly-done singing. Paul "wants both to be conjoined, provided the heart precedes the tongue."[14]

Whereas Colossians envisions musical praise as a function of internally embraced doctrine (the proper fruit of the love of truth), Ephesians sees it as outwardly expressed joy from

---

14 Calvin, *New Testament Commentaries*, ed David W. Torrance and Thomas T. Torrance (Grand Rapids: Eerdmans, 1965). 11:353.

the infilling of the Spirit. Calvin noted this distinction in his commentary on Ephesians observing that the "holy joy with which the Spirit of God gladdens us" leads us to "the pleasant and delightful fruits" of corporate singing. God wants us to be accustomed to "deep drinking" in the joy of the Holy Spirit and express it within the congregation through songs of praise in the spirit of thanksgiving. "The innumerable benefits which we receive from God yield cause of joy and thanksgiving" and thus prove an "ungodly and disgraceful laziness, if they shall not all through their life study and practice the praises of God."[15] In light of this, corporate worship involves an elevated state of energy and joyful thought; engagement of mind and heart for this most important of all human activities does not suffer the indolent lightly. Mind, heart, and mouth engaged with divine truth and grace call forth all the "heart, mind, soul, and strength" in expressions of love to God.

Worship in truth produces praise; worship in Spirit produces praise. These are not two different sources of praise, but manifest the unity of Spirit and truth in true worship. They show that word and Spirit must always conjoin if we are to worship rightly.

A Testimony in Song from Baptists

A letter produced by the Anabaptist Conrad Grebel to Thomas Muntzer chastened the recipient for having begun to use German hymnody in worship. That was not right, they believed, for singing in public worship has no warrant from the New Testament. In fact, Paul scolded the Corinthians for their chanting, as if singing, in worship and he specifically told

---

15 Calvin, op. cit., 204.

the churches in Colossae and Ephesus that "if anyone wishes to sing, he shall sing and give thanks in his heart." Moreover, Paul commanded that "the Word of Christ shall dwell in us, not singing." And one more for good measure, of practical and ethical concern, Grebel had noticed that "He who sings poorly is vexed; he who is able to sing well becomes conceited."[16] The Anabaptists rightly feared anything introduced into worship unwarranted by Scripture; wrongly, however, they misconstrued the meaning of texts that clearly encouraged, no, enjoined, singing as an element of corporate Christian worship.

Baptists arose from a movement that, like the Anabaptists, was in reaction against the use of human books to guide worship, specifically *The Book of Common Prayer.* An over-reaction to forced uniformity in worship eliminated the use of any books that guided worship except the Bible. As a result, congregational singing had no place in corporate worship for decades.

Benjamin Keach (1640-1704) was convinced that the Bible mandated singing as an element of corporate worship. This caused a controversy in his church and led to a church split between singers and non-singers. The controversy spread to other churches and led to writings that included such energetic defenses of respective positions, words that were seen as offensive, insulting, erroneous, or misrepresentative of brethren. A committee of the Baptist Association was appointed to seek to bring some order and restoration of love and respect among brethren. The committee pointed out nine offenses in the writings of Keach about certain controverted issues including singing. After consenting to the committee's judgments on the several issues, and clarifying certain words that

---

16 W. R. Estep, ed., *Anabaptist Beginnings: 1523-1533* (Nieuwkoop: B. De Graf, 1976), 33.

he felt they had misunderstood, Keach concluded that none should suppose by his consent to their observations, that "I am changed in my judgment about singing the Praises of God." In fact, the entire controversial exchange led him to be "more confirmed in it, with many others." Rather than drop the controversy, Keach said, "you may see the said Answer with some Additions reprinted, though all those things that have offended shall be wholly left out."[17]

Keach found that it was "no easie thing to break People off of a mistaken Notion, and an old Prejudice taken up against a precious Truth of Christ."[18] He noted in particular the Puritan reaction against the Anglican prescribed form of worship and wrote,

> The Lord will, I hope, satisfied all his People about this heavenly Ordinance in due time, and they shall not call it a Carnal nor a Formal thing any more, nor cry out, *'Tis as bad as Common Prayer.* I must tell them, if *Common Prayer* lay under Sacred Institution in the *New Testament*, as singing of *Psalms* and *Hymns* doth, I should as freely embrace that: But whereas the one is *Humane*, so the other is *Divine*, that is, ordained and commanded of God, as well as practiced by Christ and his disciples, and by the Saints in all ages.[19]

Keach's convictions brought him to the front of the development of a hymn literature for the church both by way of

---

17 James M. Renihan, ed., *Faith and Life for Baptists: The Documents of the London Particular Baptist General Assemblies, 1689-1694* (Palmdale, CA.: Reformed Baptist Academic Press, 2016), 112.

18 Benjamin Keach, *The Banquetting House*, (London: 1692), 11 of "To the Reader"

19 Keach, 11, 12.

theoretical argument and actual production. "We are exhorted to sing," Keach argued, "Psalms, Hymns, and Spiritual Songs, and since we have none left in Form in the Scripture, it follows, that those whom God hath gifted that way, ought to compose them; for a Hymn cannot be sung without its form."[20] If God enjoins a duty, he establishes a way. The "extraordinary Gift" of singing was not to be expected any more. At the same time, neither were sermons delivered by special revelation, but by careful construction from the word of God. Those so gifted should write hymns fit to be sung in the worship of God.

For Keach, a by-product of singing hymns was pedagogical and evangelistic. "Now these hymns being short," he observed in the preface to a book of hymns that he produced, "Children will soon get them by heart, as also full of varieties, and if instructed to sing, they may be the more affected with the matter, and receive the greater advantage"[21] Though some parts of the life of the church excluded unbelievers, such as the Lord's Supper, holy discipline, and days of fasting and prayer, other parts could be attended by the public, and to good advantage. These included "publick Prayer, Reading, and Preaching the Word, and in Singing God's Praises. . . . May others, my brethren, join in Prayer with us, and not praise God with us?"[22] He followed with fifteen reasons why corporate praise is of such a powerful and significant influence as to be a required part of the worship of God's church. In one of these he wrote, "Brethren (as a worthy divine observes) the Church in her publick Worship is the

---

20 Keach, 8, 9.
21 Keach, 5.
22 Benjamin Keach, *The Glory of a True Church and its Discipline Displayed*. London 1697), 64.

nearest Resemblance of Heaven, especially in Singing God's praises. What Esteem also had God's Worthies of old, for God's publick Worship? *My Soul longeth, yea even fainteth for the Courts of the Lord, How amiable are thy Tabernacles, O Lord of Hosts!*"[23]

His friend, Hercules Collins, came to Keach's aid in seeking restoration of this sadly-omitted element of the worship of God. Not only does singing "sweeten a prison," as it did for Paul, and "prepare a soul for suffering," as it did for Christ but "singing may be sanctified to the conviction of sinners, as well as praying and preaching is." "Praise," said Collins, "is the natural duty of all, the proper duty of saints, the perfect act of angels."[24] The unregenerate, therefore, should not be excluded from singing any more than they should be excluded from hearing the word. Even when unbelievers perform those things, however, that it is their duty to do, the doing of them still is carnal and finally unacceptable to God as pure worship. "We must sing with grace," for it is grace not nature that "sweetens the Musick" and "Grace is the root of true Devotion."[25] All worship must be done in Spirit and truth.

To make our singing accord with truth, Collins presented a defense of composing hymns based on biblical revelation and giving singable meter and language to biblical psalms. In light of the cessation of special revelation, our sole, and abundantly sufficient, source of divine truth is in the written word of God.

> But yet also I do think, that we are at our liberty to compose other parts or portions of God's word to

---

23 Keach, *The Glory*, 67.
24 Hercules Colllins, "An Appendix Concerning the Ordinance of Singing" in *Orthodox Catechism* (London, 1680), 80.
25 Collins, 85.

that end; provided our Hymns are founded directly on God's word, these very hymns may be called the Word of God, or spiritual Hymns. For, as a learned man saith, 'tis the sence and meaning is the Word of God, whether in prose, or in Meeter; and further saith, We may as well be said to sing God's Word, as to read it; it is only orderly composed and disposed for that action. Every Duty must be performed according to the Analogy of Faith, and founded on God's Word. All Prayer or Preaching, that doth not correspond with sacred Writ, notwithstanding any pretence of an extraordinary Inspiration, I am to explode out of God's Worship. And as Prayer and Preaching must correspond with the sacred Record, so must Singing; And as we count them the best Prayers and sermons, that are fullest of Scripture, so those Hymns that are founded on the sacred Scriptures, can no more be denied to be of the Spirit, than a Man's Preaching or Prayer, which is full of the Word of God.[26]

Punctilious attention to the word of truth did not inhibit Collins's understanding of the special ethos brought to worship in the proclamation of truth through song. He gave eleven aspects of the attitude that must consciously be present as the church engages to address God and praise him through singing. Not only must we sing "with understanding," but we also must "sing with zeal and affection," "we must sing with grace," and "we must sing with spiritual joy" for singing "is only triumphant gladness of a gracious heart."

This gladness that is prompted by the inner working of grace reminds us of the admonition of James, "If anyone is cheerful, let him sing praise" (5:13). God seems to have

---

26 Collins, 84.

attuned the vocal apparatus to the elevation of affection so that with the body we may express in fitting ways the exuberance, or the crushing despondency, of the soul. A shout, a groan, a sob, a song—all of these give vent to one's emotional state. Collins's concept of "triumphant gladness" raises the question of the place of lament in singing. How should it be expressed? As all expressions of confessions of sin and lowness of spirit in a felt absence of sustaining grace, they are to be countered by the conscious calling to mind of redemptive blessings—the triumph of forgiveness over guilt, eternity over temporality, hope over distress, and glorification over decay. The psalmist looks forward to the redemptive solution to his downcast soul: "Why are you cast down, O my soul, and why are you in turmoil within me? Hope in God; for I shall again praise him, my salvation and my God" (Psalm 42:11). After the darkest psalm of the Psaltery, Psalm 88 ends, "My companions have become darkness." Psalm 89, written by the same poet, Ethan the Ezrahite, begins, "I will sing of the steadfast love of the Lord, forever; with my mouth I will make known your faithfulness to all generations" (Psalm 89:1). Expressions of lament and distress, therefore, should be given in order to stir up grace and to express confidence in and dependence on the Lord's covenantal lovingkindness. Psalm 44 contains a deeply distressing recounting of the great triumphs of Israel's enemies over them to their disgrace and sense of rejection and includes the words "You have made us like sheep for slaughter and have scattered us among the nations." When Paul cited the Maskil of the sons of Korah, how does he apply it? In the full maturity of redemptive fulfillment, Paul considers all that could possibly distress and defeat the Christian and responds, "No, in all these things we are more than conquerors through him who loved us" (Romans 8:35, 36). We do not avoid lament and deeply-felt remorse for sin, therefore, but we let it give way to the "triumphant gladness of a gracious heart."

Fifth, Collins reminds us, we must "sing with faith" for it "puts pleasantness upon every duty." Given the peculiar character of this medium of worship, "We must sing with excited grace, not only with grace habitual, but excited and actual." In singing we "must stir up the grace in us" as David did in Psalm 57:7-9: "My heart is steadfast, O God, my heart is steadfast; I will sing and give praise. Awake, my glory! Awake, lute and harp! I will awaken the dawn. I will praise You, O Lord, among the peoples; I will sing to You among the nations." Though grace is sovereignly and unilaterally bestowed in in the awakening of the soul to repentance and faith, for the Christian who recognizes his dependence on it, grace may be stirred up by conscious and affectionate reflection on both the present blessings of grace and by setting our hopes "fully on the grace that will be brought to you at the revelation of Jesus Christ" (1 Peter 1:13).

Collins's seventh requirement for singing was "We must sing in the Spirit, as well as pray in the Spirit." What we sing are called spiritual songs because of their origin as Spirit-driven perceptions of the beauty and glory of what we praise. "The Spirit excits [sic] and compleats the Soul to this holy Service," Collins taught, and the singing of spiritual songs is the effect of the fullness of the Spirit. "This Wind must fill our Organs before we can make any musick." Also, we must keep our hearts when involved in this work or we can slip into an attempt to please men "with the artificial suavity of the Voice, and displease God with the odious impurity of the Heart." Nor should we neglect prayer as preparatory for singing and for all spiritual duties.

The tenth point is that in singing we must "labour to see [our] interest in Christ clear." The one who is not in Christ certainly is out of tune spiritually and thus presents an absolute dissonance in his singing. Christ alone "must put acceptation upon this service." He is the altar that sanctifies the gift even as he perfumes the prayers of the saints (Revelation 5:8). So "he must articulate their Singing." Finally, Collins envisions this heavenly scene:

> Let us sometimes raise our Hearts into holy Contemplations, let us think of the musick of the Bride-Chamber, there shall be no crackt Strings, displeasing Sounds, harsh Voices, nothing to abate our Melody; there shall be no Willows to hang our harps upon, *Psalm* 137:2. In the Bride-chamber, there shall be no sorrow to interfere. When we sing the Song of the Lamb, there shall be no Grief to jar our harmony: for which day let us all pray.[27]

Thus, it is the word of God that governs the music; music, in turn, gives soaring flight to corporate expressions of the word. If this music is set within the context of a guiding text, the musical texts not only are individual expressions of revealed truth, but in their combination serve to interpret and put to praise the passage that expresses the theme of worship.

---

27 Collins, "Appendix," 84-86.

Chapter Eight

O Had I Jubal's Lyre

"Like the sound of harpists playing their harps."
Revelation 14:2

No Uncertain Sounds

Though Hercules Collins was instrumental in the restoration of congregational singing as a mandated part of corporate worship, he was not instrumental. He found no warrant for the use of instruments in worship. Those who opposed him in his support of singing presented an objection to singing by assuming the possibility of a musical slippery slope. They all agreed that instruments were carnal; but using voices for music opened the door for instruments. He posed the objector's theoretical question, "If singing be with the Voice, why not with Lute, Harp, Organs, and other Instruments?" Our Hercules answers that the voice itself completes the purpose of redemption in the restoration of pure praise, while the non-verbal use of music typified unfulfilled prophecy and is, therefore, superseded.

1. In the New Testament the Voice and Heart are only God's instruments. The Voice is still required, because the immediate interpreter of the Heart; and tho artificial instruments are laid aside from God's worship, yet not natural ones.
2. The Union of Heart, Tongue, and voice, make the spiritual way of Worship under the Gospel compleat. We have not any thing as typical now to look at, as the Lute and Harp were in the Law, as also those Ceremonies which typed out Christ's sacrifice; but when the Substance came, the Shadow ceased. So the Spirit being more abundantly poured out, we have no need of those Instruments; but there needs Soul and Body always to sing forth the high Praises of God."[1]

Collins merely shared with the larger body of Puritans an objection, not to the private use of instruments, but to instruments in worship. Obviously, with the abundance of instruments used in the Old Testament in the praise of God, some biblical, covenantal, theological reason for their discontinuity with New Testament must be established if they are not to be allowed. Collins's reason was fairly standard—the voiceless, wordless praise of instruments must now give way to the completed revelation and work of redemption. Charles Spurgeon shared the Puritan and early Baptist objection to the use of instruments: "As for instrumental music, I fear that it often destroys the singing of the congregation, and detracts from the spirituality and simplicity of worship."[2] A common view was that the ten-stringed lyre under the hand of Christ

---

1 Hercules Collins, *Orthodox Catechism* "Appendix", 81.
2 Charles Spurgeon, *Metropolitan Tabernacle Pulpit*, XIV (1868), 141.

was fulfilled by living voices and melody from living stones in service of a living Christ. Voices now express the words of completed revelation and replace what was necessarily wordless, not fully revealed and accomplished, under the old covenant.

Are Instruments Ceremonial and Typological?

Certainly, the issue of the cessation of the sacrificial system is well-taken. Not only is it obviously typological which has a clearly defined anti-type in the work of Christ, but the case for its cessation is argued in the book of Hebrews as well as other places. For instrumental music, however, there is no obvious antitype nor is there a doctrinal exposition that renders its use an affront to the completed work of Christ. The sacrificial system came in as a positive ceremonial ordinance to remind the people that sin remained from day to day and year and year. Only the blood of a worthy victim could satisfy divine justice and assuage the guilty conscience.

Instrumental music, however, did not arise as a positive ceremonial ordinance but appears in Scripture as a natural art expressing human emotion and creativity. Its use in human society arises naturally and its use in worship is, therefore, partly natural and moral and partly positive. The first appearance of instrumental music is found in Genesis 4 in the seventh generation from Cain when one of his descendants, Jubal, is described as the "father of all those who play the lyre and pipe". His descending from Cain does not make the activity corrupted, for his brother Jabal was the "father of those who dwell in tents and have livestock." Neither the one nor the other indicates that the discovery is cursed.

What Jubal did was to discover a way of harnessing properties built into creation as one of the manifestations of the glory of God. In a way, he was subduing the earth as God had commanded Adam in his unfallen state (Genesis 1:28). When God confronted Job with the shallowness of his true knowledge of divine power in creation and its sustenance, he asked Job, "On what were its bases sunk, or who laid its cornerstone, when the morning stars sang together and all the sons of God shouted for joy?" (Job 38:6, 7). At the creation of the world the principles of music were established and operative from the time there was light on the first day. When the stars appeared as gathered light and manifested the symmetry, harmony, and complementary relationships that exist in the entire created order, the angels "shouted for joy." As light may be measured according to differentiation of frequency, so may sound. The principles in both mediums lie behind the making of music.

The discovery of music and the ever-expanding horizons of how it is produced, how harmonic effects in a continuous pattern give ever-new sources of human joy, are not harnessed by any merely ceremonial and typological partitions. They flow incessantly out of creation itself. Music is a manifestation of Trinitarian reality. Every fourth note of a chord represents a dissonance. All of us need the final resolution of tonic consonance. Perhaps this is mystical or too confident in the typological intent found in natural things, but it seems to be a witness to musical sound giving voice to the fundamental ontology of reality.

A mid-nineteenth century analyst of musical trends remarked about the recent experimentation with dissonance in both instrumental and vocal music. Likening the modish fascination with dissonance to strawberry jam that soon surfeits the palate, he wrote, "It is quite true that music would be dull and insipid without discords, but the delight which the ear experiences is not in the crash of the discords themselves, but in following their orderly motion into consonance. Consonance is the substance of music; dissonance its adornment. We never tire of plain chords, such as those in the Old Hundredth. The grandest progression in music is from tonic to dominant, or vice versa."[3] Dissonance adds lovely texture and mystery to the flow of music as well as the flow of history. It can add agitation to the experience, symbolizing the unrest we experience in a fallen world; but rest and a sense of finality are welcomed in the final resolution.

Jubal made instruments and Miriam, the prophetess, "took a tambourine in her hand, and all the women went out after her with tambourines and dancing. And Miriam sang to them, 'Sing to the Lord for he has triumphed gloriously.'" (Exodus 15:20, 21) The "Song for the Sabbath" of Psalm 92, an expression of singing accompanied by instruments, establishes timeless themes as the source of praise, themes that could just as easily be urged after the death of Christ as before it.

> *It is good to give thanks to the Lord,*
> *To sing praises to your name, O Most High;*
> *To declare your steadfast love in the morning,*
> *And your faithfulness by night,*
> *To the music of the lute and the harp,*
> *To the melody of the lyre.*
> *For you, O Lord, have made me glad by your work;*
> *At the works of your hands I sing for joy.*

---

3 J. Spencer Curwen, *Studies in Worship Music, Chiefly as Regards Congregational Singing* (London: J. Curwen & Sons, 8, Warwick Lane, E.C., 1880), 129.

The great song of redemption in Revelation unfolds in all its beauty and glory as the four living creatures as well as the twenty-four elders "fell down before the Lamb, each holding a harp, and golden bowls of incense, which are the prayers of the saints. And they sang a new song" (Revelation 5:8, 9). This is a compelling scene for understanding that instrumental music is not merely typological. They sing of the completed work of redemption through the ransoming power of the shed blood of Christ for people of "every kindred, and tongue, and people, and nation," while they play their harps. The final Lamb has been slain (5:6), but the harps are employed in the praise of that reality, "You were slain, and by your blood you ransomed people for God" (5:9). The Sons of Korah envisioned this scene in Psalm 87 when the newborn saints from every nation gather in the "city of God," the new Zion, glorying in all that were born in her while "both the singers and the players of instruments say, 'All my springs are in you'" (Psalm 87:7). The full celebration of God's restoration of chosen sinners to himself finds expression in voices accompanied by instruments.

Instruments that Prophesy

The historical objections, however, do point to a reality that needs conscientious examination and faithful execution. Clear cognitive expression and understanding is paramount in both praise and proclamation.

First Chronicles 25 lists twenty-four groups of twelve musicians who were responsible for "song in the house of the Lord" to be executed under Asaph, according to the order of King David. Included in this arrangement for orderly worship, led by competent musicians, were a number of prophesying instruments. Instruments mentioned there are cymbals, psalteries, and harps. Psalm 105 adds trumpet, lute, tambourine, strings, and pipe. The final ingredient to the praise admonished in that psalm is "Let everything that has breath praise the Lord." Human voices joined in concert with these instruments for the praise of God "in his sanctuary." The same appears to be the case in 1 Chronicles when the musicians' work supplied a context for the duty to "give thanks and to praise the Lord" (1 Chronicles 25:3).

It is striking that in the use of instruments—"with harps, with psaltery, and with cymbal"—the musicians were to "prophesy" (1). Again, in listing their names the writer noted that they "prophesied according to the order of the king" (2). Another sentence mentions six names who "prophesied with a harp, to give thanks and to praise the Lord" (3). Other sons of music leaders served "for song in the house of the Lord, with cymbals, psalteries, and harps, for the service of the house of God." Their song was accompanied with instruments.

Instrumental music was to be used in support and enhancement of the words. Heman, called "the king's seer" (5), had responsibility for determining that the text of songs was true and exalted so that the praise of God was, indeed, a word of prophecy, that is, a setting forth of divinely revealed truth, as well as an experience of exaltation of the name of the Lord (1 Chronicles 25:5, 6). These musicians were skillful in their playing and also "trained in singing to the Lord."

As in 1 Corinthians, we see the priority of prophecy. At Corinth, the prophecy consisted of new covenant truth divinely revealed to those gifted as prophets by the Holy Spirit, in the time of corporate worship. Paul warned against, in fact forbad, the use of tongues in public worship unless each utterance was interpreted, at which point it became prophecy (1 Corinthians 14:6 et al.). Under Heman, the prophecy was an accurate rendering of a psalm combining its text with an instructive setting of instrumental accompaniment. Instruction in divine truth and the practice of rational worship, structured to elevate the affections according to the understanding was the goal in both 1 Chronicles and 1 Corinthians.

In light of this connection of skill, beauty, and words as expressions of both general and special revelation, rationale to discontinue the use of instrumental music in Christian worship is slim to none. Instead, one finds a pattern of reasons to employ it tastefully in full submission to and for the exaltation of words of revelation, the prophetic word. It should be done skillfully so as not to become a distracting aggravation of soul, and it should not dominate or smother the use of words so as to become an uncertain sound unfit to prepare the saints for battle. In an interesting note to his father in May 1855, Charles Spurgeon invited him to the last service in Exeter Hall before the reopening of renovated New Park Street on May 31. He informed his father that "The organ will be played and collection will be made."[4] Probably the organ was to be used during some of the congregational singing. When used skillfully and discreetly, instruments can prophesy!

Instrumental music enhances a time of worship when it gives aid and support to words of truth that are intentionally set to meter, rhyme (or other poetic devices), and tune. Music helps us feel a rhythm that has been intentionally impressed on the words to connect emotional emphasis on the leading

---

4 Personal photo of handwritten note from the archives at the Metropolitan Tabernacle.

ideas of the text. Instrumental music supports the movement of tunes and expands our perception of how tones relate to each other, how harmony expresses the symmetry and beauty of God, and adds a dimension of expression that aids the affections in exalting the transcendent glory of a text of praise. Such use of instruments is disciplined by the word of prophecy and designed for such combinations of expression, both voice and instrument, that give free expression of praise to God for all his glorious attributes and mercies.

An intriguing combination of instrument and prophecy undergirds the theological musing of Psalm 49. The psalmist calls on all people, low and high, rich and poor, to listen to the meditation of his heart. He will introduce rich ideas of redemption and the certainty of judgment. The ransom of a soul from Sheol is more than can be managed by any mortal (7, 8) for only God can do it. These musings he calls "wisdom," he refers to them as "the meditation of my heart," and looks upon his God-induced thoughts as "understanding." Two other words show the profundity of his subject matter when he calls the thoughts a "proverb" or a "parable" and then refers to it as a "riddle" (ESV) or a "dark saying" (NKJV). Since he has called upon every level of society to listen, by what medium will he set forth these profound mysteries? How will he demonstrate that their relative class here has no bearing on their stance before God in a time of judgment ("even the wise die; the fool and the stupid alike must perish"). He will engage their attention through a song, a song accompanied by an instrument. In fact, the setting of the idea to the music of a lyre gives an added dimension of useful contemplation to this difficult idea: "I will incline my ear to a proverb; I will solve my riddle to the music of the lyre" (4).

Praise can be pleasant and worthy with only words and voices. At the time of stated worship, music falls short of true praise in the absence of words and voices. With voices, words of revelation, and instruments, praise may elevate the soul into realms of utterance and perception unparalleled in any other experience.

J. Spencer Curwen listed his credential as "Associate of the Royal Academy of Music, Certificated to Teach Harmony by the same, President of the Tonic Sol-fa College." In an examination of congregational singing in churches in London in the early 1870's, having observed the tendencies of music professionals both in writing and playing, he compared that aspect of musical production to the practice of congregational singing. His observations imply wise counsel for the combination of instruments and voices in worship.

> The fact is, these modern tunes are written to be played rather than sung. We strum them on our pianofortes, and sigh over the most beautiful of the discords. Our fingers know nothing of awkward and unvocal intervals, or of the effort and training which is needed to hold a strong dissonance with the voice. The study of the pianoforte, while it has discouraged the practice of purely vocal music, has cultivated the sensibility to musical sounds to a remarkable extent, for the mere habit of listening to music cultivates the ear. It is this wide-spread appreciation of instrumental music which has in recent years affected our psalmody.
>
> But the style of instrumental music is necessarily distinct from that of vocal; the singer and the player need different treatment. A dissonance of a semi-tone is no more trouble to play than the most ordinary

concord, but it is almost impossible to get a choir to hold it with perfect resolution and in perfect tune. The old counterpoint was born of singing rather than of playing. It comes to us from a time when instruments were feeble and imperfect, and it studied that smooth motion of the parts which is so effective in vocal harmony. The later tunes, bearing traces of the glee or the Handelian chorus, are no less distinctly vocal. Effects that are congenial to voices are studied, and what voices cannot do is carefully avoided. Now-a-days composers of hymn-tunes write for the organ, and seldom stop to consider whether what they write can be sung.[5]

Curwen observed that attention to instrumental music can help make congregations more artful and more heartful in their singing. At the same, his observation provided a warning against the tendency to use the time of corporate worship as a showcase for music as an art rather than music as prophecy.

THE NON-VOCAL INSTRUMENT—A COMPETITOR OR A COMPLEMENT

Narrative of truth in Bible reading, corporate recitation, and sermon epitomizes the content of corporate worship. Words in song reinforce the narrative and bear an independent witness through a different genre. Music through unliving things crafted in an amazing variety of forms to channel the physical presence of music all around us, as intriguing, engaging, and elevating as it is, must always be servant of

---

5 J. Spencer Curwen, *Studies in Worship Music*, 1st series, 3rd ed. enl. & rev. (London, 1901).

the text of truth and not vie for artistic autonomy. Musical solos on instruments, however, would serve the purpose of publicly proclaimed truth where the tunes are well-known and bring into play both the message of the text as well as the affection evoked in the music.

Narrative is designed by the Creator to have its own way of gaining the adherence of the mind and affections. When music is used under a narrative of revealed truth to which it is not purposefully related in rhythm, tune, and affection, it does not enhance by adding a fitting enlargement of the total effect. Rather, it muffles or competes with the prepared narrative. Narrative has a separate and intrinsic rhythm emphasizing the power of the word, logical construction, and unsung modulation of voice that must be alone to gain its unique appeal. The classic parts of well-ordered speech—logos, ethos, and pathos, with the determined avoidance of bathos—give the spoken word a power unique to itself. To hem in a narrative by an undercurrent of unrelated, often improvised, musical sounds hides the beauty of the spoken word, spoils its freshness and openness to subtle tonal spontaneity, robs it of its native power, and may even contradict its mood.

This suggested prohibition of the musical underscore to narrative, though generally to be observed, does not reach the level of an absolute. Creating a complementary and strengthening relationship between a narrative and a layer of music beneath it is a rare art but may be accomplished at times. The musical sound bed should underscore a clear verbal connection both with the themes of the narrative and the ideas within the songs to which it serves as a bridge. If not, it establishes either an alien theme or the distracting competition of non-descript plunking. That this type of mixed genre at times can serve to support a message may be seen in the sensitive, and skillful, interplay between dialogue and music in musicals. A dialogue between Marian Paroo and Harold Hill underscored by "Till there was You" increases in intensity in light of the plot and how both the words and the music of that song advance the story. Please pardon the secular example, but I use it to show how these distinct genres of communication may combine positively to concentrate the mind and the affections in specific and carefully selected cases.

The persons involved, both the narrator and the musician, should have the same commitment to enhancing the message, not highlighting the music or merely establishing a mood. They should share a virtual unity of intuition as to how truth will be clarified in the combination of narrative and instrument so that the narrative will not be challenged, hurried, intimidated, or amended by the presence of musical phrasing. No musical underscoring should be used for prayer, Bible reading (with the exceptions of the Psalms on occasions), or with a narrator who has not purposefully planned and coordinated his words with the musician so that the combination is natural and strengthening. A clumsy combination dilutes not only the integrity of the narrative but the appropriate power and usefulness of the music in a setting of worship.

Without this kind of foresight, care, and sensitivity to the principle that all must serve the purpose of truthful worship, the person hearing an intended narrative with an underswell of unrelated rhythm and chords finds difficulty in focusing on the intent of the narrative. He or she may be distracted by seeking to discern the organization or message in the music. Attention to the instruments interrupts attention to the narrative. "What is he playing? Do I recognize that line? What did the speaker just say?" Even if avoiding banal combinations of chords and flourishes, if done in the most tasteful and skilful manner, the medium itself, when not fitted for the particular type of vocal production and combinations of words and phrases, smothers the intended usefulness and power of narrative.

In a significant way, the medium is the message. Rather than an enhancement and an ordered participant in the prophetic, such a use of the skilled musician, except on the rare occasion mentioned above, renders him a distraction, a competitor for attention when all the focus should be given to the spoken word. The combination is not euphonic but rather cacophonic by pitting two discrete mediums as competitors when all hearts, minds, and ears should be led to a holy concentration on the beauty and glory of God through a medium fitted for the purpose.

Bring 'em On

God invites us to enjoy his music with as much skill and beauty as possible. The most varied and lovely instrument, the one immediately from God's hand, is the human voice. No two voices are the same; the rich timbres of human vocalization present sounds of unmatched beauty. Trumpets, trombones, clarinets, flutes, French horns, stringed instruments, pianos and keyboards—and yes, cymbals and drums—catch unique musical sounds that are not duplicated in the human voice. In their combination we honor God in bringing his own work in creation into service of the gospel. When voiceless instruments serve the interests of gospel proclamation, teaching, admonishing, and praising with a voice of song, the splendid variety, rhythm, and sound they add catch the wind of gospel beauty and make a habitation for God to visit his people.

Chapter Nine

Giving

"See that you excel in this act of grace also."
2 Corinthians 8:7

"The minister who mixes giving in with the gospel offends his people and loses his credibility with them," so opined one of the senior members of a Bible study group. "He should stick to the Bible and spiritual things and not make visitors think that all the church is after is their money." Ill-prepared food leaves a bad taste in the mouth; a master chef can encourage the palate for more. Giving, wrongly approached and wrongly perceived, can seem merely a carnal interest. Giving, seen in the biblical framework of divine sovereignty and the restoration of praise, can seal to the soul a transcendent approach to life and worship.

Excel In this Act of Grace Also (2 Corinthians 8:7)

All that God sets forth as constituting the grace of worship culminates in the restoration of praise. An important element of New Testament worship is the giving of material possessions in recognition of our dependence on God and his abundant provision for us. This part of worship should be practiced with both humility and gladness. Worship leaders need not apologize about its presence in worship, for it is mandated in Scripture, has abundant examples of its practice, and shows the miraculous operation of God in turning our material wealth, a thing that could be wicked mammon, into spiritual gain.

Jesus told a parable, recorded in Luke 16:1-13, about a shrewd manager of another's wealth who learned to turn the money of his master into friendship for himself. Having mismanaged the funds initially, he reduced the debt to all those in debt to his master. When they paid, they felt indebted to the steward for giving them a substantial break, a favor that made their lives much more manageable. In this way, the conniving manager created a great system of hospitality for himself when his boss released him. Jesus made application of the surprising words of the rich man: "The master commended the dishonest manager for his shrewdness." Jesus then recommended the principle to his followers, "And I tell you, make friends for yourselves by means of unrighteous wealth, so that when it fails they may receive you into the eternal dwellings."

Material possessions represent the energy, stewardship, and values of our lives. In a marvelous spiritual alchemy, Jesus, through the gospel, turns material gold into spiritual riches. Learning to treat these material advantages properly is a strong measure of spiritual maturity and perception. An abundance of grace and the desire for the praise of God to fill the earth powerfully affects the believer's life of worship in his attitude toward giving. For this reason, it is a constituted part of corporate worship.

LOVE OF MONEY

Having money, even in abundance, has no trace of evil in it. The Proverbs indicate that the gaining of wealth is the outcome of industry, patience, honesty, talent, generosity, and faith (Proverbs 11:24; 12:11; 13:11, 22; 21:20; 22:29) Conversion restores this deep sense of faithful labor to life that will result in discretionary income (Ephesians 4:28). The use of wealth can be an expression of abundance of love to others and grace from God (Luke 19:8-10). Poverty can be the result of mysterious providential arrangements to test and form the character of some people and offer opportunity for demonstration of compassion for others (Acts 4:34-37). Poverty also can arise from slothfulness and indiscretion (Proverbs 13:18; 24:30-34; 28:22). Others gain wealth by dishonesty, greed, stinginess, covetousness, oppressiveness, and brutality only to see their lives lost in the process (Proverbs 22:16, 22, 23). Jesus warned against covetousness, for a "man's life consists not in the abundance of the things that he has" (Luke 12:15).

The use of money can show one's love for God; on the other hand, love for money can indicate a heart attached to this perishable world rather than to imperishable inheritance in heaven. The writer of Hebrews warned that one must "Keep your life free from the love of money, and be content with what you have." (Hebrews 13:5) In the same spirit Paul warned Timothy about the spiritual devastation that can issue from the love of money. "But those who desire to be rich fall into temptation, into a snare, into many senseless and harmful desires that plunge people into ruin and destruction." The folly to which one may be driven in his quest for money not only will destroy his joy and stability and fragment his relationships in this world, but shut his eyes to the permanence of peace, beauty, and satisfaction in the knowledge of God here and hereafter. "For the love of money is a root of all kinds of evil. It is through this craving that some have wandered away from the faith and pierced themselves with many pangs" (1 Timothy 6:9, 10).

The Bible sets forth the remedy for this danger, not in the pursuit of poverty, but the practice of generosity in using wealth to create spiritual strength and enhance one's vision of the satisfaction of eternal life. Riches in themselves do not provide us with anything; but God, who created all things and sustains his people, faithfully grants us all that we need for life and godliness: "His divine power has granted to us all things that pertain to life and godliness, through the knowledge of him who called us to his own glory and excellence" (2 Peter 1:3). For that reason, Paul urged Timothy to give these striking words to the rich.

> As for the rich in this present age, charge them not be haughty, nor to set their hopes on the uncertainty of riches, but on God, who richly provides us with everything to enjoy. They are to do good, to be rich in good works, to be generous and ready to share, thus storing up treasure for themselves as a good foundation for the future, so that they may take hold of that which is truly life" (1 Timothy 6:17-19).

Wicked mammon when filtered through a pure heart may become treasure stored up in eternity. Love of money keeps us from giving. The regular practice of giving is, in fact, the spiritual means for mortifying the fleshly temptation of covetousness against which we are warned so severely (Ephesians 4:5) and which rides so easily on the coat-tails of increased wealth (Luke 12:20, 21). The restoration of praise to the heart focuses our love on God and his glory. This new affection unlocks our feverish grasp on worldly status through money to pursue instead the cause of God and truth. Even money, therefore, takes its place in the way God's people worship together.

Pragmatic Reasons for Giving

The Bible presents us with many practical needs that God intends to be met by the generosity of his people. God intends for employers to pay fair wages (James 5:4-6), He expects those who have wealth to meet the needs of those who are "poorly clothed and lacking in daily food" (James 2:15-17). John reinforces this with his admonition "But if anyone has the world's goods and sees his brother in need, yet closes his heart against him, how does God's love abide in him? Little children, let us not love in word or talk but in deed and in truth" (1 John 3:17,18). Proverbs points to the blessedness of the one "who is generous to the poor." The one who "oppresses the poor insults his Maker, but he who is generous to the needy honors him" (Proverbs 14:21, 31). Scriptures on this issue could be multiplied but these show us that meeting the needs of the poor evidences the genuineness of love, expresses true faith, honors God as Creator, and unfolds the reality of grace in the heart. So tied are material things to spiritual truth that our use of them gives virtually infallible evidence of one's spiritual state.

Without giving, churches will have great difficulty in maintaining an adequately prepared and competently maturing gospel ministry. Without reservation, existentially and historically informed appreciation for bi-vocational and non-compensated ministers of the gospel comes from all quarters of the Christian world. The biblical ideal, however, historically verified, is that a church should provide livable compensation for a preacher of the gospel to function according to the tasks required of him in Scripture, including the call that he be hospitable. Benjamin Keach listed one of the duties of a congregation toward a pastor as provision of "a comfortable maintenance for them and their families, suitable to their state and condition." [1] Keach included this in the church covenant adopted at the constitution of the church meeting in White-Street in 1696. This would be the church served 150 years later by Charles Spurgeon. The article stated, "We promise according to our ability (or as God shall bless us with the good things of this world) to communicate to our pastor or minister, God having ordained that they that preach the gospel should live of the gospel."[2] This should be done "cheerfully with all readiness of mind" so that their sustenance is as comfortable under grace as the Levite's was under law. Paul referred to this comparison in 1 Corinthians 9:14, "In the same way [like the provisions for the Levites through the sacrifices of the people of Israel], the Lord commanded that those who proclaim the gospel should get their living by the gospel."

The securing of the presence of ongoing gospel ministry for ourselves and our children, as well as the lost around us, should be a matter of first priority and approved wholeheartedly as a deeply spiritual activity. This idea undergirds

---

[1] Benjamin Keach, *The Glory of a True Church, and its Discipline Display's* (London: 1697), 14.
[2] Keach, 74.

Paul's instruction in Galatians 6:6, "One who is taught the word must share all good things with the one who teaches. Do not be deceived; God is not mocked, for whatever one sows, that will he also reap." Remarkably, as Paul continued his argument, he likened the use of money to the sowing of seed. The one who neglects this kind of sharing, or works of benevolence, sows to the flesh and will reap corruption. The one who remembers to use his wealth to support the teaching of the word sows to the Spirit and "will from the Spirit reap eternal life." This intensely pragmatic concern bears fruit in a deeply spiritual outcome.

Giving is the divinely ordained means for supporting the extension of the gospel in the world. Though Paul worked often to support himself and knew both how to abound and how to suffer want, he expressed deep gratitude for financial support when it came and saw it as a spiritual work on the part of the giver. "It was kind of you to share my trouble," he wrote the Philippians, and noted that they alone had "entered into partnership with me in giving and receiving" (Philippians 4:14, 15). As he told the church at Corinth, he had not burdened them with any demand for support but "robbed other churches by accepting support from them" when they sent brothers with a gift and thus "supplied my need" (2 Corinthians 11:8, 9). The ease with which Paul passed from acknowledging the material help he received into the spiritual life reflected in such giving is vitally instructive. Their gift to him was, at the same time, "fruit that increases to your credit." His receipt of "full payment" so that he found himself "well supplied" meant that they had presented a "fragrant offering, a sacrifice acceptable and pleasing to God" (Philippians 4:18).

The apostle John looked upon giving toward gospel extension in the same way Paul did. When he wrote to his generous friend Gaius, he commended his willingness to work for the propagation of the gospel through traveling missionaries. In 3 John 5-8, John said, "Beloved, it is a faithful thing you do in all your efforts for these brothers, strangers as they are, who testified to your love before the church." Note that the hospitality and generosity of Gaius was a true expression of obedience to the faith and a manifestation of his love. "You will do well," John continued, "to send them on their journey in a manner worthy of God." He was not to be begrudging, or skimpy, close-fisted in his support, but filled with grace, generosity, and a desire to reflect the goodness of God in his gift. As an element of his rationale for encouraging this support, John reminded Gaius, "For they have gone out for the sake of the name, accepting nothing from the Gentiles." Their motivation for going was God-centered, expressly gospel-centered, and they expected to receive nothing from those to whom they went to preach the gospel. John completed his combination of gratitude and exhortation with a note of spiritual oughtness—"Therefore we ought to support people like these, that we may be fellow workers for the truth." Spurgeon had absorbed this truth and taught his peers this lesson: "We are persuaded the bait of 'No collections' is needless and demoralizing. To teach men to give of their substance for the spread of the gospel is a part of the gospel, and tends greatly for their own benefit."[3] Monetary support in such an effort to sustain and expand the circumference of gospel knowledge and influence makes the giver a fellow worker for the truth.

---

3 Charles Spurgeon, *The Sword and the Trowel*, November 1879: 545.

The Connection of Grace, Praise, and Giving

As seen above in the admonitions of the apostles and as expressed in our Lord's parable about the unjust steward, giving on the basis of Christian conviction and for the increase of gospel preaching gathers spiritual fruit. Giving flows from and expresses praise to God. As we remember that "Praise is his gracious choice," we see that we discipline ourselves away from the "love of money" and toward the "fragrant offering" and acceptable sacrifice by considering giving as an ordained element of worship. Paul emphasized this aspect of giving in his appeal to the Corinthians to contribute to the material needs of the suffering Jewish Christians in Jerusalem. He used the Christians of Macedonia as an example. "Their abundance of joy and their extreme poverty have overflowed in a wealth of generosity on their part" (2 Corinthians 8:2). Of joy they had abundance, of material means they had little, but the combination "overflowed in a wealth of generosity." It was generous, because it arose from little (as did the widow's giving in Luke 21:4), and it was an overflow of true wealth for it came from an abundance of joy. As joy undergirds praise, and giving is itself prompted by joy, so giving must be engaged as a meaningful element of corporate worship.

Paul went on to describe the sense of praise and gratitude that prompted the giving of the Macedonians: "For they gave according to their means, as I can testify, and beyond their means, of their own free will, begging us earnestly for the favor of taking part in the relief of the saints" (2 Corinthians 8:3). In closing his lengthy discussion of this aspect of Christian worship and discipleship, Paul produced a virtually seamless description of giving and the grace that restored generosity to the heart. Again, employing the analogy of giving as the sowing of spiritual seed, Paul wrote, "Whoever sows sparingly will also reap sparingly, and whoever sows bountifully will also reap bountifully." This is a matter of personal discipleship, expressing love for one's neighbor and delight in God as the great Giver, for "each one must give as he has made up his mind, not reluctantly or under compulsion, for God loves a cheerful giver." The act of giving, however, as seed-sowing, becomes a multiplier of grace, for, "God is able to make all grace abound to you, so that having all sufficiency in all things at all times, you may abound in every good work." Continuing the analogy, Paul linked generous giving to an abundant harvest of the most profound spiritual blessings: "He who supplies seed to the sower and bread for food will supply and multiply your seed for sowing and increase the harvest of your righteousness."

How expansively Paul had grasped the meaning of Jesus' parable about the alchemy that changes wicked mammon to eternal benefits may be felt when he insisted, "You will be enriched in every way for all your generosity, which through us will produce thanksgiving to God." Money becomes praise, "for the ministry of this service is not only supplying the needs of the saints, but it is also overflowing in many thanksgivings to God." When the recipients of this gift actually see it, benefit materially from it, and recognize it as evidence of real love and unity in Christ, both the giver and the recipient are bound together in exuberant worship to the greatest giver of all. "By their approval of this service," that is, the evidence of love demonstrated in this service, "they will glorify God because of your submission flowing from your confession of the gospel of Christ," that is, their honor of Christ in this offering manifests the truth of their orthodox confession of his redemptive Lordship. Exuberant love and faith produced "the generosity of your contribution for them and for all others," and, in return made them "long for you and pray for you" as a result of "the surpassing grace of God upon you."

From the love of money, givers are transformed into lovers of God and of people, and that which was a stumbling block has become the smooth path to renewed and exuberant praise. Such exalted laudation of the power of giving is no hyperbole in this Pauline message but a fitting description of what it means to emulate our saving Lord: "Thanks be to God for his inexpressible gift" (2 Corinthians 9:6ff).

Praise through Giving Is His Gracious Choice

The time of giving in corporate worship—and it should certainly be a part of corporate worship—should be given a setting of genuine praise. The place of giving should not be hidden from view and the event itself should not be shrouded as if covered with an apology. While God hates ostentation and display (Matthew 6:1-4), he loves a cheerful giver. Giving can be celebrated as one of the most profound aspects of the restoration of praise to life without creating a situation that enhances pride or encourages partiality. To give for the increase of gospel proclamation in the world, to give for the relief of pain and distress, and to give for sustaining a worshiping community is itself a gift from God stirred up in the heart by grace.

Under the principle of Scripture-guided worship, the time of giving frequently will arise in direct and explicit response to the guiding text. In all cases, a worshipful response of giving is implicit throughout the biblical revelation.

The psalmist had observed that many to whom God gave splendor in earthly possessions and wealth he also took out of this life with all of their riches, their glory, left behind. "Do not be afraid when one becomes rich, when the glory of his house is increased; for when he dies he shall carry nothing away; his glory shall not descend after him" (Psalm 49:16, 17). In light of the grace of divine transformation, how should one use the "glory" with which he has been blessed in this life? (Psalm 30:11, 12)

> *You have turned for me*
> *My mourning into dancing;*
> *you have loosed my sackcloth*
> *And clothed me with gladness,*
> *That my glory may sing your praise*
> *And not be silent.*
> *O Lord my God,*
> *I will give thanks to you forever!*

Our glory, both non-material and material, is given that it may sing the praise of God. "We now sing the praise of God with both heart and hand through the grace of giving."

Chapter Ten

THE ORDINANCES

"So those who received his word were baptized.... And they devoted themselves to the apostles' teaching and the fellowship, to the breaking of bread and the prayers."
Acts 2:41, 42.

JESUS REMINDS US

Under the authority of Christ, the church practices two ordinances, baptism and the Lord's Supper. Both of these are proclamations of the chief aspects of the covenant of redemption in accordance with which Christ was crucified (Romans 6:3; Matthew 26:28; 1 Corinthians 11:25). In his baptism, Jesus foretold that his obedience to the Father would lead him to a bloody death. In the Lord's Supper, Jesus established a remembrance of his abused body and bleeding wounds just prior to their infliction.

The ordinances of baptism and the Lord's Supper manifest the Trinitarian character of the covenant community, the church, and the specific trinitarian rhythm that should always be present in the witness of corporate worship. As does the entire revelation of the New Testament, these ordinances set forth a vigorous Christocentric trinitarianism.

These ordinances do not highlight themselves as sources of salvation but point to the historical work of Christ when he bore our sins in his own body on the tree. They are solemn and serious proclamations of the central facts of the gospel always to be enacted in the context of explanation and proclamation. Their power is not primarily existential, but they draw attention to the finality of the historical redemptive event. In doing so, they remind us that all spiritual blessings flow to us from the consummated ransom of Calvary.

The ordinances teach us submission to the governing authority of the revealed word of God. Participation in them calls for a mental and spiritual embracing of their truth. Each directly affirms the worship of God in Spirit and in truth. Only the Spirit qualifies a person to receive them; and only by the word of God does the Spirit change our minds and fit our hearts to bear in our bodies their reality. By the word of God we learn the truth, and by the Spirit of God we confess the truth that Jesus is Lord and receive the mercies resident in his resurrection from the dead (1 Corinthians 12:3; 1 John 4:2; 5:1;1 Peter 1:22-25; Romans 10:8-13).

There is no room for guess-work in interpreting these symbols. Though they are symbols, they are clearly interpreted symbols. Though they are short dramas, they have a prescribed meaning. God certainly is not opposed to the expressive power of symbol and drama and has designated these two enactments of the victorious passion of Christ as the church's *play*.

Every vital aspect of plot, character, conflict, resolution, and denouement makes deep impressions on the entire participating community as the church regularly enacts the drama of redemption. We see man as fallen and under the curse of death with nothing he can do to release himself from its verdict. He is under the threat of eternal death, and moreover is oblivious to the roiling waters of divine vengeance ready to surround him. He comes to himself; we sense the difficulty of an awakened conscience in futile efforts to reverse this just sentence, and we struggle with the helplessness of man. We learn that an eternal covenant has been arranged just fit for this situation, expressive of the eternal wisdom, immutable justice, and invincible love of God. As designated in this covenant, the only person who can possibly rescue these sinners appears. He accomplished the work necessary for salvation through unimaginable cost: a conflict with the unbelief of those he came to save, an extended contest with the arch-fiend, the devil, and, most wrenching, he places himself in the stead of those who should receive from the Father "indignation and wrath, tribulation and anguish" (Romans 2:8, 9), a cost that none but that one could pay. The covenant involves the shedding of blood, the beating of his body, an entombment behind a sealed rock. His hard work is rewarded by his Father, he rises from the dead with such abundance of approval that eternal spiritual blessings accrue to all those who trust his work, and his work alone, for their acceptance before God. They are given the promise of eternal life, hope in this life, a renewal of soul to love and reach for holiness, and a sense of final resolution through the kingly return of their suffering servant.

A solemn but lively presentation of each ordinance helps each participant and observer enter the perfection of these ultimately true dramas. They are the dominically warranted proclamations of the real story that do not call for speculation as to their meaning. Their meaning is repetitively pressed on the mind and heart of the community. Their repetition draws us, not to the drama itself or to the elements that bear the story, but to its once-for-all divine enactment historically "in his body on the tree" as interpreted authoritatively in the present day according to divine revelation.

These ordinances do not operate as mere appendages to corporate worship, stuck on or pressed in with clumsiness or without connection to the entire experience, but reflect the essence of body life. They are so vital in expressing the particular event that has given the church existence, that they must constitute, along with the appropriate concentration on the word, the substance of the church's confessional witness in worship whenever they are celebrated. They embody the singularity and absoluteness of the truth, "There is one body and one Spirit—just as you were called to the one hope that belongs to your call—one Lord, one faith, one baptism, one God and Father of all, who is over all and through all and in all" (Ephesians 4:4-6).

Baptism

Jesus commanded his disciples immediately before his ascension, "As you go make disciples of all nations, baptizing them in the name of the Father and of the Son, and of the Holy Spirit" (Matthew 28: 19).

They obeyed His command according to His instructions: Exactly according to his word, we find the disciples at Pentecost responding, "So those who received his word were baptized" which consisted of "everyone whom the Lord our God calls to himself" (Acts 2:39, 41). We find the same order true in Samaria, "But when they believed Philip as he preached good news about the kingdom of God and the name of Jesus Christ, they were baptized, both men and women" (Acts 8:12). When the gospel came with power to the house of Cornelius through the preaching of Peter, in the presence of the "believers from among the circumcised," Peter declared, "Can anyone withhold water for baptizing these people, who have received the Holy Spirit just as we have?" On that basis, therefore, "He commanded them to be baptized in the name of Jesus Christ" (Acts 10:47, 48). When the Philippian jailer heard the message, "Believe in the Lord Jesus, and you will be saved, you and your household," he took Paul to his house where Paul and Silas "spoke the word of the Lord to him and to all who were in his house" (Acts 16:31, 32). The promise of salvation through faith was to him and to his household, so they too must hear the word in order to believe. They did and "he was baptized at once, he and all his family." The last part of verse 34 should read, "And he rejoiced, all of his house having believed in God." The whole household was instructed in the word, the whole household believed, and the whole household was baptized.

Baptism is Trinitarian. In the baptism of Jesus (Matthew 4:13-17), we see the clearly trinitarian arrangement of the ordinance. The Son of God is there, submitting to all righteousness; the voice of the Father is there proclaiming the belovedness and the eternal sonship of the Son; and the Holy Spirit is there descending as a dove showing that, in this mysterious incarnation, the Son of God himself must indeed fulfill all righteousness as a man who "through the eternal Spirit offered himself without blemish to God" (Hebrews 9:14).

Immediately after this initiatory event and the manifestation of the trinitarian nature of this mission, the continuing element of the Spirit's involvement becomes clear. Jesus was "full of the Spirit" and was led, really driven, by the Spirit into the wilderness to be tempted of the devil. This began the tests in which Jesus fulfilled all righteousness that we might be justified and adopted.

For us, baptism reflects the work of the Spirit both in fitting us for union with Christ by regeneration and empowering us for "newness of life," that is, sanctification. He unites us with the Lord Jesus in his perfect work of salvation, and testifies to our place as a member in the body of Christ, the church. "For just as the body is one and has many members, and all the members of the body, though many are one body, so it is with Christ. For in one Spirit we were all baptized into one body . . . and all were made to drink of one Spirit" (1 Corinthians 12:12, 13). This is one reason that baptism is so closely tied to church membership. All of the "members of the body" bear witness that they too were "made to drink of one Spirit," that is, have been subject to the saving operations of the Spirit, and were placed by the Spirit, not only into the universal church composed of all the elect of all ages, but into this local congregation. There, by the gifting of the Spirit, we work "for the common good" (1 Corinthians 12:7).

Baptism also draws attention to the powerful operation of the Father in raising Christ from the dead – "having been buried with him in baptism, in which you were also raised with him through faith in the powerful working of God, who raised him from the dead" (Colossians 2:12). Again, Paul inserts the operation of the Father into the meaning of baptism in writing, "We were buried therefore with him by baptism into death, in order that, just as Christ was raised from the dead by the glory of the Father, we too might walk in newness of life" (Romans 6:4). Baptism signifies that Christ is the "firstborn among many brothers," and as we have followed him in his death so we are released from "bondage to corruption and obtain the freedom of the glory of the children of God." We are sons of God through faith in him and the Father has received us as his children.

When Paul explained the meaning of our baptism ("as many of you as were baptized into Christ") as the expression of our having "put on Christ" (Galatians 3:27), he gave a pungent summary of the trinitarian foundation of salvation. Under the initiatory authority of the Father in the eternal covenant of grace, he sent the Son. By this work of redemption, the Father then sent the Spirit. "But when the fullness of time had come," that is, the time established in eternity when the Father gave to the Son a people to save (John 17: 3, 4), "God sent forth his Son," that is, at the precise moment that the "power of the Most High" (Luke 1:35) overshadowed Mary, "born of woman," for in addition to the overshadowing of the Most High the Holy Spirit had come upon her so that child was both Son of God and son of Mary born of her flesh, "born under the law," that is, truly born as a Jew under ceremonial law and as the Son of Man under the moral law, "to redeem those who were under the law," because the law held us captive to its true moral demand of death to the transgressor, "so that we might receive adoption as sons" for when the legal barriers are removed by his suffering he "is not ashamed to call [us] his brothers" (Hebrews 2:12). "And because you are sons," So Paul continued, "God" that is, God the Father according to the terms of the covenant and on the basis of the reconciling work of Christ, "has sent the Spirit of his Son into our hearts, crying, 'Abba Father!'" This new familial status means "you are no longer a slave, but a son, and if a son, then an heir through God" (Galatians 4:4-7). All of this meaning is invested in the putting on of Christ in the public testimony of baptism. The triune God is on our side, for us in mercy. The entire congregation, before whom this is done, remembers, confesses, testifies to the same understanding, and worships.

Baptism points to a finished work. One's baptism signifies that he is bearing witness to the finished work of Christ and has taken to himself all that is implied in having been bought with a price. He confesses, as it were, "I do know that my body is a temple of the Holy Spirit within me, whom I have from God. I am not my own, for I was bought with a price. So henceforth, this body that has been buried and has risen again with Christ will be put to the service of the glory of God" (1 Corinthians 6:19, 20). To "put on Christ," therefore, as a voluntary act of obedience to the command of Christ is to reflect the work of Christ immediately, for when we are baptized we are "baptized into his death" (Romans 6:3).

Christ's death is the event that embodies all things that lead the sinner from death to eternal life. It sets in motion the powers brought to bear on the sinner to carry him from under the curse to the glorified state in heaven. From our being foreknown in Christ, to our being called, justified, sanctified, glorified, and appearing in his image before all the citizens of heaven, all flows in a never-ending stream from his death. "He who spared not his own Son, but delivered him up for us all, how shall he not also, along with him, freely give us all things" (Romans 8:32). Baptism symbolizes that, testifies for the person and the church that vital truth, presses the historical reality on the conscience, and leads the church, not to rely on the symbol, but to confess more deeply their dependence on the Savior in his once-for-all work (Hebrews 7:26-28).

Baptism denotes identification with Christ's suffering. Though baptism does not activate God's saving work but symbolizes its content, that does not mean that nothing existential is at stake at all when a person submits to the ordinance. When disciples asked about their place in his kingdom, Jesus pointed to the fact that only through a baptism in blood and the emulation of it in the life of the disciples would the kingdom be established. "Are you able to drink the cup that I drink, or to be baptized with the baptism with which I am baptized?... The baptism with which I am baptized, you will be baptized" (Mark 10:38, 39). Christ's obedience to this baptism of ransom blood would seal and mature his unbroken course of righteousness to the Father's will (Matthew 3:15 – "Thus it is fitting for us to fulfill all righteousness"). In this baptism, he announced that, because of this perfected righteousness (Hebrews 5: 8, 9), after a baptism in blood (Mark 10:38-45), he would be raised from the dead.

Those elements of redemptive truth, present when Jesus was baptized by John the Baptist, define for us what should be present both in our minds and in the accompanying words during the practice of this ordinance. By entering into John's baptism, he affirmed John's message about Jesus himself and also the reality of sin in the human family and the need for repentance. Though he was sinless, he took on himself the debt of sinners. As we are baptized in water as he was, so we are committed to take up the cross, follow him, and be willing to be baptized in blood as he was. Having been brought to faith, we testify publicly that Christ's life, death, and life-again is ours. Again, to this Paul pointed when he wrote the Galatian churches, "for in Christ Jesus you are all sons of God, through faith. For as many of you as were baptized into Christ have put on Christ" (Galatians 3: 26, 27). In baptism, the person announces that he has counted "all things as loss because of the surpassing worth of knowing Christ Jesus my Lord and, in order that I may know the power of his resurrection, I now show my commitment to share in his sufferings and become like him in his death" (cf. Philippians 3:8, 10).

It is not a time for light banter or humorous observation but a time for being committed to the resurrection of the righteous through dying the death of the righteous. It denotes that Jesus, being set apart by the Father for such a death, also consecrated himself for this death, that those given to him by the Father would be forgiven of sin and be granted eternal life by His righteousness. Our voluntary submission to this ordinance, following upon personal repentance and faith, therefore, means that we have submitted to the biblical principle that the life dependent on his death comes "that those who live might no longer live for themselves but for him who for their sake died and was raised" (2 Corinthians 5:13). In his death, we died; in his resurrection, we live. Our true life, moreover, is but for a commitment of willingness to die in the cause of the Christ who bought us with his precious blood.

THE LORD'S SUPPER

The gospel writer Luke (22:19) recorded, "And he took the bread, and when he had given thanks, he broke it and gave to them saying, This is my body, which is given for you. Do this in remembrance of me. And likewise the cup after they had eaten, saying, This cup that is poured out for you is the new covenant in my blood." We find that the first church "devoted themselves to the apostles' teaching and fellowship, to the breaking of bread and to prayers" (Acts 2: 42). This ordinance was to be practiced by the whole church as a matter of deep solemnity and in demonstration of gospel unity.

The manner and mental attitude in partaking is important: To reinforce that fact, Paul gave a sober warning to the Corinthian church about her attitude and conduct in the time of corporate worship when partaking of the memorial meal: "For as often as you eat this bread and drink the cup, you proclaim the Lord's death until he comes. Whoever, therefore, eats the bread or drinks the cup of the Lord in an unworthy manner will be guilty of profaning the body and blood of the Lord. Let a person examine himself, then, and so eat of the bread and drink of the cup. For anyone who eats and drinks without discerning the body eats and drinks judgment on himself" (1 Corinthians 11:26-29). Solemn warning, indeed, and intended to discourage any reception of the Supper not permeated with both Spirit and truth.

As an established perpetual element of corporate worship, the memorial should be approached with understanding. There must be no extortion of the heart in exalting the material of the Supper beyond biblical warrant. At the same time, it must not be demoted from its ordained place to effect sanctifying meditation on the redemptive work of the cross.

Symbols in Perpetuity – In the text in Matthew 26:26-29, Jesus used the words "Take, eat; this is my body." Also with the cup he said, "Drink of it, all of you, for this is my blood of the covenant, which is poured out for many for the forgiveness of sins." Some traditions receive these words as indicating that there is a perfect identity between the elements partaken and the body and blood of Christ. Roman Catholic theology asserts that transubstantiation takes place. The elements, maintaining all the appearance, feel, and taste of bread or wine actually become the real flesh of Christ and the true blood of Christ. This miracle of "transubstantiation" occurs at the use of the appropriate form by the priest and those partaking receive grace *ex opera operato*, that is, in the very act of taking, unless the recipient has committed mortal sin. Lutheran liturgy upholds a doctrine of "real presence" but not transubstantiation. Because of Christ's omnipresence, and through the words spoken, Christ's body and blood, united in one person with his deity, actually are present in the elements of the Supper, so they believe.

Although Zwingi and Calvin differed in some matters of expression, they agreed in this, "Hence, any man is deceived who thinks anything more is conferred upon him through the sacraments than what is offered by God's Word and received by him in true faith."[4] Zwingli wrote of eating both spiritually and sacramentally. To eat spiritually was to receive the work of Christ by faith in that God has promised forgiveness through the death and resurrection of his Son to those who receive that work as the only means by which sinners can be reconciled. To eat sacramentally occurs when "you join with your brethren in partaking of the bread and wine which are the tokens of the body of Christ.... You do inwardly that which you represent outwardly."[5]

As an expression of disgust, some have characterized the Zwinglian view as that of "bare symbol." If one means by bare, that no importance for spiritual growth and deepened worship of Christ is intended by it, then the word "bare" is a complete caricature. If one means that the elements add

---

4 John Calvin, *Institutes of the Christian Religion*, ed. John T. McNeill, trans. Ford Lewis Battles (Louisville: Westminster John Knox Press, 1960, 2006) 2:1290.

5 Huldreich Zwingli, "An Exposition of the Faith," in *Zwingli and Bullinger*, trans. G. W. Bromiley (Philadelphia: The Westminster Press, 1953), 259.

nothing to the reconciling transaction that was accomplished in time and space in the body of Christ on the cross, then the word "bare" is a truly evangelical affirmation. The bread and wine are symbols, naked and unadorned, and do nothing but point, but point with sober poignancy, to the place where all was done.

The biblical narrative supports the idea that this is the use of a symbol by Jesus. Jesus often used the verb of being to speak of a symbol that depicted some aspect of his redemptive work. "I am the door of the sheep" (John 10:7). John, in fact, called this manner of teaching a "figure of speech" or a "similitude" (10:6) "I am the true vine" (John 15:1). At Passover, Jews would say, "This is the bread of affliction," meaning it symbolizes the affliction they had endured in Egypt. Jesus' words, therefore, recalled this emblematic power already present in the Passover meal.

The historical reality is that Jesus stood before them and had not yet had his body broken nor his blood shed. He called the wine ("this is") the "blood of the covenant which is poured out for many for the forgiveness of sins." That blood had not yet been shed, for, in accord with the covenant, it would be shed, poured out, but once to accomplish forgiveness. The book of Hebrews gives clarity that the reality of that historical event cannot be duplicated; in fact, it need not be duplicated for in completing the covenantal provisions it was sufficient once and for all (Hebrews 7:27; 9:12, 15, 24-28; 10:9, 10, 14, 18; 13:20, 21).

The symbols are to remind us of the perfect satisfaction provided by Christ in his once-for-all death on the cross. They do not draw attention to themselves as having any efficacy, but to the single event in which reconciliation occurred. He poured out his blood for many and in that death he brought to justification the many for whom he died: "By his knowledge my righteous servant shall justify many, for he shall bear their iniquities... He poured out his soul unto death... He bore the sin of many, and made intercession for the transgressors" (Isaiah 53:11,12).

If the disciples partook of his actual body, as yet unbroken and unbruised, did they partake of his mortal, unresurrected, unglorified body, or did they partake of the body that did not yet exist? Do we partake of the same body that they did, if in fact we take his literal body? Do we partake of the body as it was before his resurrection or after his resurrection? Or does Christ still have both a mortal body capable of death and a glorified body incapable of death? Or is this more likely symbolic language that draws our adoration to the great redemptive transaction on Calvary? For that purpose, he took on a body that he might die in our nature to give eternal life to our nature: "Sacrifices and offerings you have not desired, but a body you have prepared for me; ... I have come to do your will, O God.... And by that will we have been sanctified through the offering of the body of Jesus Christ once for all" (Hebrews 10:5-10). The body that was offered once satisfied forever for the forgiveness of sins and the sanctification of the believer. That body was glorified in the resurrection, and never will be offered again.

Salvation comes not through any kind of intrinsic efficacy in the material elements of bread and wine themselves; rather it resides in the satisfaction of divine wrath justly manifested in time and space on one of our race who could lawfully, ontologically, and morally stand in as our substitute. Jesus was morally qualified to suffer vicariously for he had no transgression of the law as his own for which he must die. He was truly man and stood as our covenant head. He had a human body, a human mind, a human spirit all of which must endure fully the divine wrath due his people. This he did during his hours on the cross and finished the suffering. No more will his blood be shed nor his body broken. His life was poured out with his blood on the cross and there is no occasion in which the blood of the covenant must be poured out again.

It is a memorial. The passages in Luke 22 and in 1 Corinthians 11 point to the reality that, in partaking of the Lord's Supper, we remember what he did. Luke 22:19 recorded the words, "Do this in remembrance of me" after the giving of the bread. In 1 Corinthians 11:23-26, Paul gives a straightforward presentation in which he records Jesus using the words of remembrance after both the bread and the wine. After breaking the bread, Jesus said, "This is my body which is for you. Do this in remembrance of me." When he took the cup he said, "This cup is the new covenant in my blood. Do this, as often as you drink it, in remembrance of me."

As they were taking the Passover, Jesus gave a simplified partaking of elements. The Passover had been predictive and prospective. Their partaking of the lamb was to serve as a promise of redemption. The yearly celebration reminded them of the promise, that God would provide a lamb in the future who would take away the sins, not of the Jews only, but of the world. As Jesus instituted the Lord's Supper, he presented it as a memorial. Its future celebrations would look to that which already was accomplished and was retrospective of the past work of Christ. This symbolic drama was to be surveyed by the heart in calling to mind the greatness of the sacrifice. Each recipient can say with Isaac Watts, "When I survey the wondrous cross on which the Prince of Glory died, my richest gain I count but loss, and pour contempt on all my pride."⁶ The element of the prospective was reinserted as we now look to the coming-again of the Lord in his glorified body. As the supper points to faith in that which has been done in his body, so it points to hope in that which will be done in our body: "But our citizenship is in heaven, and from it we await a Savior, the Lord Jesus Christ, who will transform our lowly body to be like his glorious body, by the power that enables him even to subject all things to himself" (Philippians 3:20, 21). "Christ, having been offered once to bear the sins of many, will appear a second time, not to deal with sin but to save those who are eagerly waiting for him" (Hebrews 9:28).

We do not look to the elements of which we partake at that moment as having redemptive significance in themselves, but only as they point us to the historic, time-space sacrifice of Christ. The symbols call us to look to Christ himself, presently interceding for us on the basis of the blood he shed at Calvary. In remembering, the participants actively press their minds to recall the biblical presentation of the historic event of redemption. This memorial presents an objective assurance that, once for all, Christ endured the portion of wrath due to them, so that "in him we have redemption through his blood, the forgiveness of sin" (Ephesians 1:7).

This event in the worship of the church is a time of proclamation of the gospel, for "we proclaim the Lord's death until he comes." It is a time of preaching the gospel to our own souls for we partake of bread and wine in active remembrance of Jesus as the only redeemer. We do this in a sense of worship, with reverence, and repentant humility for this must be taken in a worthy manner lest we betray a heart that yet has

---

6 Isaac Watts, "When I survey the Wondrous Cross," *The Baptist Hymnal*, Hymn # 144.

not felt the gravity of Christ's sacrifice and we remain, not redeemed, but "guilty concerning the body and blood of the Lord." It is, therefore, a time of sober examination, calling for deep discernment of the reason that Christ was given a body, a necessary sufferer in our stead. It is not a time for the careless or curious, the one merely fascinated by the quaintness of the process, but for the body of believers to "come together" to worship the one who underwent judgment for us.

SCRIPTURE-GUIDED WORSHIP

Given that the symbolism resident within the ordinances touches a theme that is biblically pervasive, many texts in the Bible, well-distributed throughout, could lead to a meaningful application of it in pointing to the ordinances. Supposed for example, the text for the sermon was Revelation 11:16-18. "And the twenty-four elders who sit on their thrones before God fell on their faces and worshiped God, saying, 'We give thanks to you, Lord God Almighty, who is and who was, for you have taken your great power and begun to reign. The nations raged, but your wrath came, and the time for the dead to be judged, and for regarding your servants, the prophets and saints, and those who fear your name, both small and great, and for destroying the destroyers of the earth." The worship leader selected as the guiding passage for the liturgical expression of truth, Psalm 138:4-8.

All the kings of the earth shall give you thanks, O LORD,
*   for they have heard the words of your mouth,*
and they shall sing of the ways of the LORD,
*   for great is the glory of the LORD.*
For though the LORD is high, he regards the lowly,
*   but the haughty he knows from afar.*
Though I walk in the midst of trouble,

> *you preserve my life;*
> *you stretch out your hand against the wrath of my enemies,*
> *and your right hand delivers me.*
> *The LORD will fulfill his purpose for me;*
> *your steadfast love, O LORD, endures forever.*
> *Do not forsake the work of your hands.*

One may easily see the powerful parallels within these two passages and how the guiding text gives rise to the several elements of worship. In verse 7, which begins "Though I walk in the midst of trouble, you preserve my life," the emphasis of baptism on death, burial, and resurrection can be seen as a profound exposition of that very thought—trouble, but life preserved. Or perhaps for that day the Lord's Supper is to be observed. The middle of verse 8, "Your steadfast love, O Lord, endures forever" gives a broad field within which to speak of the manifestation of steadfast, covenant love in the death of Christ and the prospect of his glorious return to reign forever.

Trust in the sufficiency of Scripture. Focus on the reality that Scripture interprets Scripture. Let worship arise from the richness of the biblical text and experience both form and freedom under its guidance.

Section Three

Coherence in Truth and Practice

Chapter Eleven

HISTORIC DOCTRINAL DEFINITIONS

"The full knowledge of everything that is in us for the sake of Christ."
Philemon 6

Because modes of worship have developed along theological lines historically, one aspect of worshiping in Spirit and in truth involves a knowledgeable commitment to orthodox and evangelical doctrines as they were formed in the fires of doctrinal controversy. Two of the most important spheres in the historical delineation of biblical doctrine are Christology and salvation. These two issues obviously have unbreakable implications each for the other. From the first five centuries Christian thinkers and councils sorted many of the biblical ideas on God, Trinity, and Christ and established a creedal history that is wise to take with deep respect. The Reformation era gave renewed emphasis to issues of salvation. Through a thick forest of controversy and opposition, they forged a series of interconnected doctrines that looked to Christ and his completed work alone for salvation. This was granted through the channel of pure unmerited favor, grace alone. It terminated on individuals who received it through a simple trust in its goodness, necessity, and sufficiency, that is, by faith alone. The final purpose of the entire transaction was to point to the infinite perfections and goodness of God in justice, holiness, righteousness, faithfulness, mercy, lovingkindness, and grace, that is, to the glory of God alone. In both these spheres of doctrine, Trinitarian theology and Reformation soteriology, churches should ensure that their corporate worship, in all of its aspects, sounds a clear and discernible note.

"I Know that the Lord is Great" (Psalm 135:5)

THE GOD OF THE BIBLE IS A THREE-PERSONED GOD.

He is one God, "infinite, eternal, and unchangeable in his being, wisdom, power, holiness, justice, goodness, and truth."[7] He is simple, pure, deity, "a most pure spirit, invisible, without body, parts, or passions"[8] He is self-existent and immanent. He is utterly non-dependent on anything outside of himself for his being. He is indivisible so that he exists as himself throughout eternity as well as through all ages; beyond all created things which live and move and have their being in him, he even transcends the entirety of the created order of existence. Each person of this single deity is of this eternal, unitary, simple, infinitely glorious essence while thriving within himself as a vibrant, loving, communicating, joyful company of three persons. Each as God exists eternally with distinctive and incommunicable properties of personhood fit for their revealed internal relations of Father, Son, and Holy Spirit.

---

7 *The Baptist Catechism*, question 7
8 *Westminster Confession of Faith*, Chapter 2, paragraph 1.

The doctrine of the Trinity pervades the Bible with a haunting holiness from beginning to end. On the basis of the Bible's authority we confess of the three Persons, "the glory equal, the majesty coeternal," while "neither confounding the persons nor dividing the essence."[9] Without controversy, this vital truth, though clearly revealed, embodies profound mystery. It stands as a glorious peculiarity of Christianity. This is our God, and the truth of his three-personed eternality must always be sustained in corporate worship.

MODALISM MISSES THE TRUTH.

One attempt to rationalize this mysterious, but profoundly clear, teaching of Scripture is called modalism. This view, given its highest degree of sophistication in the teaching of two men, Sabellius and Praxeas, taught that Father, Son, and Holy Spirit were merely names that denominated three different modes in which God manifested himself in different economies of working his purpose of redemption. The interpretive burden this scheme places on a large number of biblical passages, as well as the soteriological clumsiness it creates, shows its deeply flawed, and heretical, outcome. Just a couple of examples must suffice. In addition to the extensive implications of John 14-16, two passages that relate precisely to the importance of trinitarianism as opposed to modalism are Acts 2:32-34 and Romans 8:1-11.

In Acts 2:32-34, Peter preached the first Christian sermon by pointing to the fitting roles of the Father, the Son, and the Spirit in the economy of salvation and the inter-relationships of each person. "This Jesus God raised up, and of that we are all witnesses. Being therefore exalted at the right hand of God, and having received from the Father the promise of the

---

9 *Athanasian Creed*

Holy Spirit, he has poured out this that you yourselves are seeing and hearing." It is impossible grammatically for these three to be the same person. Nor do the different aspects of the work of redemption allow it. How can Jesus be exalted at the right hand of God if he is the same person as the Father? What a misleading superfluity such a statement would be! If the three names all refer to the same person, how can one invest human language with meaning if he maintains that the one who receives the promise, the one who gives what is promised, and the substance of the thing promised all are the identical entity? How can "this Jesus" pour out the Spirit while at the right hand of the Father if he is the same person as the Spirit and the Father?

Paul's description of life by the Spirit in Romans 8:1-11 poses the same difficulty for modalism. Here we see all three persons of the Trinity operating in distinctive roles toward the same end of salvation for the believer. The Spirit, operating out of the moral necessities of the work of Christ, gives life and sets us free from the immutable principle that sin necessarily brings death. Why? Because God the Father sent his Son in our nature and in that nature condemned sin by assuming our place under that law of sin and death. In doing so, he fulfilled the righteous requirement of the law. On account of that, the Spirit draws us to Christ and gives us union with him in his saving work. Our body still dies because of sin but the outcome of bodily death is eternal life guaranteed by the meritorious work of Christ and the indwelling of the Spirit. How can one make the Father, Son, and Spirit in the relations set forth in this passage be one person? "If the Spirit of him who raised Jesus from the dead dwells in you, he who raised Christ Jesus from the dead will also give life to your mortal bodies through his Spirit who dwells in you" (Romans 8:11).

Trinitarianism is the very soul of the Christian message of salvation. There is no biblical salvation and, therefore, no biblical worship apart from submission to this truth. "The unity in Trinity, and the Trinity in Unity, is to be worshipped."[10] All of our praying, singing, speaking, preaching, and giving must be done in conscious acclamation of the reality that we have been brought to know, praise, and propagate the knowledge of the triune God, filled with beauty overflowing in saving purpose.

JESUS IS TRULY HUMAN.

An early heresy called Gnosticism denied the reality of Christ's humanity and true suffering. This led to the development of the rule of faith and eventually the Apostles' Creed. John the Apostle wrote against an incipient Gnosticism in his first letter as he insisted that a true knowledge of God involved the confession "Jesus Christ has come in the flesh." The one who did not confess *that* Christ is not of God (1 John 4:2, 3). One of the points of the confession referred to by Paul in 1 Timothy 3:16 has the line, "He appeared in flesh." John wrote in his gospel, "The word was made flesh and dwelt among us" (John 1:14). Peter said, "He himself bore our sins in his own body on the tree" (1 Peter 2:24). Even after the resurrection, Jesus demonstrated that, though now glorified, his body still was substantial (Luke 24:38-43; John 20:26-28).

Ignatius, bishop of Antioch in Syria was led to Rome in chains by soldiers in the year 112. He went there to die—and to die with a deep sense of privilege to shed his own blood in witness of his love for and trust in Christ. He was keenly

---

10 *Athanasian Creed.*

aware of heresy lurking around and sometimes within the churches; accordingly, he issued a warning to avoid those who denied the true flesh and true blood of Jesus. "I want to forewarn you," he wrote to the church at Magnesia, "not to get snagged on the hooks of worthless opinions but instead to be fully convinced about the birth and the suffering and the resurrection, which took place during the time of the governorship of Pontius Pilate. These things were truly and most assuredly done by Jesus Christ, our hope, from which may none of you ever be turned aside."[11] [157] When Marcion argued that the attribution of real flesh and real human life to the Son of God was shameful, Tertullian responded, "The Son of God was born: shameful, therefore there is no shame. The Son of God died: absurd, and therefore utterly credible. He was buried and rose again: impossible, and therefore a fact."[12]

This threat of denying the reality of Christ's humanity led to the incremental development of the *Apostles' Creed* from the earliest of the apostolic fathers until the finalized text of the Apostles' Creed appeared in the work of Pirminius (d ca. 753) in AD 750. It begins in creation and ends in life everlasting. It is trinitarian and points to forgiveness of sins, the church and the resurrection of the body. Its main emphasis, however, concerns the necessity of Christ's true human nature suffering in time and space for our salvation. "Who was conceived by the Holy Ghost, born of the Virgin Mary, suffered under Pontius Pilate; was crucified, dead and buried: He descended into hell: on the third day he rose again

---

11 *The Apostolic Fathers*, Trans J. B. Lightfoot and J. R. Harmer; Edited and revised Michael Holmes (Grand Rapids: Baker Book House, 1989), 96.

12 Tertullian, *On the Flesh of Christ*: 4, 5 in Henry Bettenson, *Early Christian Fathers* (Oxford: Oxford University Press, 1974) 125.

from the dead, ascended to heaven, sits at the right hand of God the Father Almighty, thence he shall come to judge the living and the dead."[13]

JESUS IS TRULY DIVINE.

Jesus is God. Arius, a presbyter in North Africa, claimed, around AD 318, that Jesus the Christ was not God but the first of all created things. He avoided modalism by affirming that Jesus was personally distinct from the Father and he avoided Gnosticism by affirming that he had a true human body and truly suffered. Jesus did not have a human soul and mind, however, but the created Logos inhabited the human body to give it rational energy. Moreover, not only was he distinct from the Father in person but he was distinct from the Father in essence; in fact, he was of a different essence from the Father. In other words, Arius's proposed savior shared neither our nature nor God's nature; he was neither God nor man. This was a miserable failure in giving definition to Christology.

The church throughout the Roman empire entered a period of intense clarification of language undergirding concepts that gave a defining confessional status to the biblical doctrine of Christ's deity. Thomas had been plain enough in bowing before Jesus, calling him, "My Lord and my God" (John 20:28). John, in warning against false teachers ended his first letter: "We are in him who is true, in his Son Jesus Christ. He is the true God and eternal life; Little children, keep yourselves from idols" (1 John 5:20, 21).

---

13 John H. Leith, ed. *Creeds of the Churches* (Richmond: John Knox Press, 1973), 24.

A confession that clearly affirmed this biblical truth was presented. Athanasius joined his bishop, Alexander of Alexandria, in leading the way for giving a positive presentation of biblical concepts about Christ. These affirmations not only would say what is true about Christ, but would clearly eliminate any possibility of Arius's followers finding a way to approve the confession. The worship that is due to the one who accomplished our salvation could only be given to one who is God.

The creed to be adopted had to be clear, forthright, and exclusive of any heresy on this point. A creed that endorsed ambiguity would only perpetuate substantial disharmony, lead to constant dispute, and, most importantly, endorse a principle of idolatry. Lack of pristine clarity would capitulate to the impression that Scripture itself was not clear in its christological focus. The wisdom of God would be impugned for leaving us with contradictory views on the status of the one he called "My beloved Son." What could be more absurd in Christianity than to leave the christological issue a matter of opinion, ambiguity, and diverse formulation?

Starting with a baptismal confession of faith used by Eusebius of Caesarea, the Alexandrians suggested several phrases that were indeed adopted. To the phrase "begotten from the Father," the council added the phrase "from the substance of the Father." This means that the Son's existence is not an act of the will of the Father at a point outside his own eternity but that God is eternal in his paternity and, thus, eternal in Sonship. A second phrase added to the words "God from God," the clarifying words, "true God from true God." In an age susceptible to consent to a multiplicity of deities in a pagan culture, any concept of a deity subordinate in essence was eliminated. Because begotten of the substance of the Father, his deity is a true deity. Third, in teasing out the idea of begottenness a bit more, a defining two-word phrase was added to clarify the idea of what it means to be begotten: "begotten" was followed by "not made." To beget another is a different reality from creating. That which is begotten shares the nature of the begetter. God as a begetter relates to his only-begotten as Father to Son, sharing the same eternal attributes while also maintaining eternally distinguishing traits of personhood. For this reason, the doctrine of eternal generation is a pivotally important biblical idea. Fourth, the council adopted the affirmation that the Son is of "one substance with the Father." If he is begotten of the substance of the Father this determines that he is "true God of true God." His begottenness can in no way be construed as createdness. It is not only appropriate, therefore, but necessary that the term translated *same essence*, substance, nature, be affirmed of the Son. Fifth, in light of the strange anthropology of Arius, the creed attached to the phrase "was made flesh" the exegetical comment "was made man" so as to reaffirm the true humanity of Jesus the Christ.

The creed also affirmed that it was "for our salvation" that he took our humanity into his eternal Sonship. Had he, the Eternal Son of God, not assumed our nature, he could in no wise be our savior. He could not have lived for us in order to grant us his righteousness; he could not have died for us to bear our load of sin, guilt, and punishment. "The free gift by the grace of that one man Jesus Christ abounded for many" (Romans 5:15).

JESUS IS ONE PERSON.

In 451 at Chalcedon, a council reaffirmed the full deity and full humanity of Christ but clarified the important point that this Redeemer subsisting of two natures was, nevertheless, one person, the distinction of natures not being lost by their unity in the Person. Were the Redeemer not God, no work he could do would be sufficient as a ransom matching the assault upon the honor, dignity and infinite perfections of God's righteousness. Were the Redeemer not man, he would have no warrant to act in the stead of the offending party to pay for him what is due and to do for him what must be done to merit eternal life. The Redeemer must, therefore, be one person adequately qualified to settle the case in favor of God's honor and at the same time ontologically and morally connected with those in need of redemption. Such a person was Jesus the Christ. None but Jesus will do. How could it be otherwise when a heavenly scene of worship includes this exclamation of praise: "Worthy is the Lamb who was slain, to receive power and wealth and wisdom and might and honor and glory and blessing!" (Revelation 5:12)?

THE HOLY SPIRIT IS GOD.

After half a century of controversy on this issue, during which time Arianism actually gained adherence for a brief period, the theology of Nicea was reaffirmed at Constantinople in 381 with the adoption of an expanded creed that included the deity of the Holy Spirit, affirming, "And I believe in the Holy Spirit, the Lord, and Giver of Life, Who proceedeth from the Father [and the Son], Who with the Father and the Son together is worshipped and glorified, Who spoke by the Prophets." How could it be otherwise when Paul wrote,

"These things God has revealed to us through the Spirit. For the Spirit searches everything, even the depths of God" (1 Corinthians 2:10); and Jesus taught that the Spirit "will glorify me, for he will take what is mine and declare it to you. All that the Father has is mine; therefore I said that he will take what is mine and declare it to you" (John 16:14,15). The Spirit reveals the deep things of God, things impossible to be known by a mere creature. The Spirit is perfectly adequate to take the covenantal relationship between Father and Son, settled in eternity, and declare it to the disciples. Only a party to that same covenant could do so.

Grace is Manifest in Praising the Three-in-One.

If redemption is the restoration of praise arising out of the gracious choice of God, the leader of corporate worship must find ways to affirm these powerful and glorious truths about this one who is Son of God and Son of Man and set it within an omnipresent Trinitarian rhythm. Though the ideas are deep and may bewilder the one who seeks to understand, serious and earnest efforts to worship in Spirit and in truth surely call on us to find ways to express our hope in a manner consistent with these doctrines, including the distinct orthodox language.

One of the historic manifestations of worshipful application of this revealed truth about God was composed by Aurelius Clemens Prudentius (348-410) who lived during the doctrinal turmoil and development of these times. His beautiful hymn, "Of the Father's Love Begotten," was written to place before the worshiping community a recitation of the truths that had restored such praise to their lips. The translation is by H. W. Baker and J. M. Neale.

1 Of the Father's love begotten
ere the worlds began to be,
he is Alpha and Omega —
he the source, the ending he,
of the things that are, that have been,
and that future years shall see
evermore and evermore.
2 O that birth forever blessed,
when a virgin, blest with grace,
by the Holy Ghost conceiving,
bore the Savior of our race;
and the babe, the world's Redeemer,
first revealed his sacred face,
evermore and evermore.
3 This is he whom seers in old time
chanted of with one accord,
whom the voices of the prophets
promised in their faithful word;
now he shines, the long-expected;
let creation praise its Lord
evermore and evermore.
4 Let the heights of heaven adore him;
angel hosts, his praises sing:
powers, dominions, bow before him
and extol our God and King;
let no tongue on earth be silent,
every voice in concert ring
evermore and evermore.
5 Christ, to you, with God the Father
and the Spirit, there shall be
hymn and chant and high thanksgiving
and the shout of jubilee:
honor, glory, and dominion
and eternal victory
evermore and evermore.[14]

---

14 "Of the Father's Love Begotten," *The Baptist Hymnal*, Hymn # 251.

"His Steadfast Love Endures Forever" (Psalm 136:1-26)

The Protestant Reformation of the 16th century reclaimed a biblical position on another set of doctrines and consequently produced another set of confessions of faith. The prominent doctrines developed as correctives to Rome's sacramentalism, that is, grace conveyed through the matter and form of seven practices from baptism to last rites. The Reformation focused on salvation through Christ alone, by faith alone, prompted by grace alone. Grace operates immediately on the mind and heart as the Spirit of God applies the word of God according to the purpose of God bringing spiritual and rational transformation to the elect of God. In this radically different perception of the operation of grace, the Reformation recovered the fundamental authority for all worship and doctrine as Scripture alone. A worship regimen, therefore, that regularly highlights these distinctive Reformation doctrines as a matter of praise serves the principle of worshiping in Spirit and in truth.

The principle of Scripture alone will be addressed in the next chapter. Here we want to look briefly at the Reformation concepts of Justification by Faith and redemption through Christ alone.

Justified: To stand justified before God, one must have a complete and perfected righteousness attained through a perfect obedience to the law (Romans 2:13; Romans 7:10; Galatians 3:12). The context of these same Scriptures shows us that any point of disobedience brings death, the justly threatened consequence of disregarding God's righteous requirements. Fulfillment of this life-giving, but soul-cursing, law demands death for any disobedience, and perfect and loving obedience if the promise of life is to be forthcoming. Jesus Christ has by his death paid the penalty of our disobedience thus procuring forgiveness (Ephesians 1:7). At the same time, that death sealed his entire life of perfect obedience and merited eternal life by his righteousness (Romans 5:18-21). Forgiveness is procured once-for-all in the death of Christ; our warrant to eternal life comes through the imputation of his righteousness to us. "The wages of sin is death, but the free gift of God is eternal life through Christ Jesus our Lord" (Romans 6:23). This doctrine is summarized succinctly in the *Augsburg Confession of Faith* (1530).

> Men cannot be justified before God by their own strength, merits, or works but are freely justified for Christ's sake through faith when they believe that they are received into favor and that their sins are forgiven on account of Christ, who by his death made satisfaction for our sins. This faith God imputed for righteousness in his sight (Rom. 3, 4). . . . And the Gospel teaches that we have a gracious God, not by our own merits but by the merit of Christ, when we believe this.[15]

Consistent with this, the Westminster *Larger Catechism* defines justification:

> Justification is an act of God's free grace unto sinners, in which he pardoneth all their sins, accepteth and accounteth their persons as righteous in his sight; not for any thing wrought in them, or done by them, but only for the perfect obedience and full satisfaction of Christ, by God imputed to them, and received by faith alone.[16]

---

15 *The Book of Concord* trans and ed. Theodore G. Tappert (Philadelphia: Fortress Press, 1959), 30, 31.

16 *Westminster Confession of Faith*, (The Publications Committee of the Free Church of Scotland, 1976), 163.

In Christ Alone: This concept of justification presses before us the glorious picture of Jesus Christ, not only in his mysterious person as the God-man, worthy of all praise for his very being, but particularly as the sin-bearer and righteous one by whose merit we have eternal life. "My hope is built on nothing less than Jesus' blood and righteousness."

The finality of the work of Christ presents the Christian with a Christ-centered worship in which we find the glory of the Trinity. The *Second London Confession,* chapter 22 paragraph 2 states, "Religious worship is to be given to God the Father, Son, and Holy Spirit, and to Him alone; not to angels, saints, or any other creatures; and since the fall, not without a mediator, nor in the mediation of any other but Christ alone." No saints interceding, no sacraments intervening, no human works interfering, no human authority interrupting.

TRUSTWORTHY SAYINGS

Corporate worship misses one of its major elements unless these truths consistently and persistently saturate the proclamations of the gathering. We pray with confidence of being heard only because of the completed work of Christ (Romans 8:34; Ephesians 1:17; 1 John 2:1, 2), in the power and interpretive knowledge of the Spirit (Romans 8:26), that all the covenantal blessings intended by the Father's decree (Ephesians 1:3,4; Hebrews 13:20, 21) may become the common property of all those gathered in Christ's name (Ephesians 3:17-19; 4:15, 16; 2 Thessalonians 1:11, 12). We read Scripture with confidence that it gives us a message about the triune God we serve through the redemptive work of the Son of God and that it will lead us to express our praise in Spirit and in truth (2 Timothy 2:8-10); we preach with the intent that the triune God will be glorified in our statement of his truth and that others will be drawn to join our submission to him and our glory in him (Romans 16:25-27); we sing and we confess together these vital truths for we want the words of our mouth and the meditations of our hearts to be acceptable in the sight of the one who is our Strength and our Redeemer (Psalm 19:7-14). We give as stewards of grace that this revealed, redemptive truth of God may cover the earth as the waters cover the sea (Isaiah 11:9).

In the context of the stewardship of trans-temporal truth, perceived with clarity by many who have gone before us, we join with saints above and saints across the aisle and across the globe, and give vent to the devotion of our hearts infused by the work of the Holy Spirit when we make corporate confession of truth. This is vital to worship.

Portions of the *Heidelberg Catechism* are recited by many in Christian communities during corporate worship. Its question and answer format lends itself to corporate affirmation. In addition, its content is central to biblical truth, particularly on the issues treated in this chapter, and its prose is elegant and memorable. It provides, therefore, a good model of how this practice could be incorporated into worship in any evangelical congregation. An entire congregation easily could join in affirming these answers concerning the person of Christ derived by the authors of the Catechism from parts of the Apostles' Creed.

> Q. What is the meaning of *Conceived by the Holy Spirit, born of the Virgin Mary?*
>
> A. That the eternal Son of God, who is and continues true and eternal God, took upon him the very nature

of man, of the flesh and blood of the Virgin Mary, by the operation of the Holy Ghost, so that he also might be the true seed of David, like unto his brethren in all things, sin excepted.

Q. Why was it necessary for Christ to suffer death?

A. Because, by reason of the justice and truth of God, satisfaction from our sins could be made no otherwise than by the death of the Son of God.

Q. What comfort is it to you that Christ shall come again to judge the quick and the dead?

A. That in all my sorrows and persecutions, with uplifted head I look for the self-same One who has before offered himself for me to the judgment of God, and removed from me all curse, to come again as Judge from heaven; who shall cast all his and my enemies into everlasting condemnation, but shall take me, with all his chosen ones, to himself, into heavenly joy and glory. [17]

---

17 *Heidelberg Catechism* in *Creeds of Christendom*, Philip Schaff ed., (Grand Rapids: Baker Book House, 1969), 3: 319, 320, 324.

Chapter Twelve

TENSIONS THAT KEEP US STRAIGHT

"Praise Him according to His excellent greatness."
Psalm 150:2

From the factors that we have discussed in the preceding chapters, I want to attempt a definition of liturgy; that is, a coherent and principial statement that informs the way we organize corporate worship.

> Liturgy is a formal structure given to corporate worship to bring the body to worship the Triune God through the finished work of Jesus Christ by organizing mandated practices and epitomes of divine truth in a way most conducive to instruction in the word, adoration of God, proclamation of the gospel, and sanctification of the whole body of believers.

"A threefold cord is not quickly broken," so the Preacher said (Ecclesiastes 4:12). Three strands strengthen and appropriate tensions from three directions keep a thing straight. Corporate worship developed within the framework of necessary freedom and regulated form produces the right beauty, structure, and order consistent with biblically sound, God-glorifying worship.

Three Interacting but Cooperative Tensions

Because worship is a horizontal response to vertical reality, rationally conceived liturgy is necessary. Corporate worship expresses movement between this horizontal dimension and the vertical precedent that has initiated it. Liturgy, in line with the definition given above, denominates the human organization of the revealed elements conducive to worshiping the triune God. In order to give the fitting place to each element in any given gathering of the church, the worship leader should develop a sense of order, decency, beauty, symmetry, and rhythm in structuring each service. In one sense, such structure is a work of art that gives prominence to the simple intrinsic grace and beauty of each part of worship.

Having succumbed to dullness, lack of hearty participation, and minimization of transforming instruction, liturgical studies underwent substantial examination and significant revival of interest in the last part of the twentieth century. A call led by Pius X early in that century for more lay participation in singing and more frequent taking of the sacraments in Roman Catholicism led to broader interest in the subject. A Catholic conference meeting in Belgium in 1909 expressed a view of the liturgy as *"a primary means to instruct people in the true meaning of faith and life, and the best source for nourishment in the faith."* This focus was open enough to engage other traditions in considering the opportunity for revitalization through this recumbent organ of worship.[18] Through the twentieth century the growth of liturgical study and emphasis on renewal through liturgy led to the summoning of Vatican II. Many Protestants also developed a liturgical approach to worship, sometimes influenced by the ecumenical movement, but also increasing the sacramental overtones. Some of this was sparked by efforts to escape the casualness, apparent irreverence, unsettling lack of form, and sometimes pure foolishness engendered by worship practice of the misnomered non-liturgical, free churches.

The patterns into which these attempts at lack-of-structure fall remind one of the complaint that Spurgeon brought against his own congregation as he considered some of the off-putting elements of the prayer meeting. He compared the non-liturgical prayer of his free-church style with those of the *Book of Common Prayer.*

> Christian men, who object to forms of prayer, will nevertheless use the same words, the same sentences, the identical address at the commencement, and the exact ascriptions at the conclusion. We have known some brethren's prayers by heart, so that we could calculate within a few seconds when they would conclude. Now this cometh of evil. All that can be said against the prayers of the Church of England, which were many of them composed by eminent Christians, and are, some of them, as beautiful as they are Scriptural, must apply with tenfold force to those dreary compositions which have little virtue left, since their extempore character is clearly disproved.

---

18 For example, see Cheslyn Jones, Geoffrey Wainwright, Edward Yarnold, eds., The Study of Liturgy (New York: Oxford University Press, 1978). Also, Frank Senn, Christian Liturgy (Minneapolis: Fortress, 1997).

Oh, for warm hearts, burning with red-hot desires which make a channel from the lip in glowing words; then, indeed, this complaint would never be made, — 'What is the use of my going to the prayer-meeting, when I know all that will be said if So-and-so is called on?' This is not an uncommon excuse for staying away; and, really, while flesh is weak, it is not so very unreasonable a plea; we have heard far worse apologies for greater offences. If our (so-called) 'praying men' drive the people away by their constant repetitions, one-half at least of the fault lies at their door.[19]

In their break with Rome, and eventually with the legal structures of Anglicanism, the Puritans nevertheless recognized the need for form consequent upon a thorough knowledge of Scripture. In the *Directory for the Public Worship of God*, they wrote of their desire to give "some publick testimony of our endeavours for uniformity in divine worship." They chose a course to "hold forth such things as are of divine institution in every ordinance; and other things we have endeavoured to set forth according to the rules of Christian prudence, agreeable to the general rules of the word of God" so that there would be a "consent of all the churches in those things that contain the substance of the service and worship of God; and the ministers may be hereby directed, in their administrations, to keep like soundness in doctrine and prayer."

Even amid the free displays of immediate revelatory gifts at Corinth, Paul closed a lengthy discussion giving apostolic regulation to that phenomenon with the admonition, "So,

---

19 Charles Spurgeon, *Spurgeon's Prayers* (Ross-Shire, Scotland: Christian Focus Publications, 2017), 184.

my brothers, earnestly desire to prophesy, and do not forbid to speak in tongues. But all things should be done decently and in order" (1 Corinthians 14: 39, 40).

Meaningful, truth-centered worship demands thoughtful organization. This involves devoted and educated awareness of the overall purpose of worship—a clear manifestation of the glory of God. Achieving that end means giving due attention to the relative importance of each individual part, the contours by which the parts may move together as a whole, and a sense of how this organization and movement pursues with intention and beautiful symmetry a worthy expression of praise to the triune God.

This is the first tension—"Let all things be done decently and in order."

Though worship is a horizontal response, the source of its content is Scripture Alone. It is governed by the vertical invasion of divine revelation. Nothing is to be admitted that arises strictly from tradition or naked human ingenuity or opinion; nothing should be given perennial authority in the church that inhibits the free operation of the word of God week by week. God-called ministers are given the stewardship of saturating the time of worship with the riches of scriptural revelation.

Revisiting the Puritans can help us understand the importance of this specific tension. They rejected the *Book of Common Prayer*, not because it lacked form, order, beauty, and regular reading of Scripture. As noted above, Spurgeon himself testified to this. In fact, when it first was introduced it was the occasion of rejoicing because "the mass, and the rest of the Latin service being removed, the public worship was celebrated in our own tongue: many of the common people also receive benefit by hearing the Scriptures read in their own language, which formerly were unto them as a book that is sealed." Eventually it became an offense, however, because of the repeated forms of prayer, the ceremonies practiced unwarranted by Scripture, and the similarity that some parts had to the Roman Catholic Mass. Over and above this, the Prayer Book encouraged an "idle and unedifying ministry, which contented itself with set forms made to their hands by others."

At the same, while it encouraged indolence, it discouraged gifted men with scriptural knowledge and godly intentions from entering the ministry because of their conscientious objection to many elements of the form of worship required by law week in and week out. In addition, the Prayer Book inhibited their functioning as ministers of their own flock according to their present needs and the particular relevance of the word of God. While they valued order and simplicity, they found discretionary room allowed in Scripture for the peculiar gifts and sanctified wisdom of each local pastor. They needed "some help and furniture" but not such a rigid form that they would become "slothful and negligent in stirring up the gifts of Christ in them." Under the authority of Scripture, therefore, and not of any humanly stipulated form, "each one, by meditation, by taking heed to himself, and the flock of God committed to him, and by wise observing the ways of Divine Providence, may be careful to furnish his heart and tongue with further or other materials of prayer and exhortation, as shall be needful upon all occasions."[20]

The leader of worship has, therefore, specific items of

---

20 "The Directory for the Publick Worship of God," in *The Westminster Confession of Faith* (Inverness: The Publication Committee of the Free Church of Scotland, 1976), 373, 374.

content that God has established that are to be managed within the general biblical principles of worship. Pastoral insight into the peculiar needs of the congregation and the implications of the sermonic text give rise to varieties of content in prayer, selections of Scripture to be read, words and style of music, the inclusion of catechetical or confessional material, and the particular place of the ordinances and giving.

Within the framework of *sola scriptura*, therefore, the Puritan wing of the late Reformation era found both its form and its freedom in worship. *Sola Scriptura* provided the perfect freedom from the commandments and traditions of men which bound the conscience and practice to ideas and actions that God had never commanded. Paul gave a pungent statement about the oppressiveness of "human precepts and teachings" in Colossians 2:16-23 and 1 Timothy 4:1-5. At the same time, they could have perfect confidence that if they followed Scripture they would be found worshiping God while truly and consistently increasing in the knowledge of God. As Paul wrote, "If you put these things before the brothers, you will be a good servant of Christ Jesus, being trained in the words of the faith and of the good doctrine that you have followed" (1 Timothy 4:6).

Ulrich Zwingli (1484-1531) stated in his writing *Of the Clarity and Certainty of the Word of God*, "We should hold the Word of God in the highest possible esteem . . . and we should give to it a trust which we cannot give to any other word. For the Word of God is certain and can never fail. It is clear and will never leave us in darkness. It teaches its own truth. It arises and irradiates the soul of man with full salvation and grace."²¹ John Calvin (1509-1564), after describing the manner and content of Reformed worship, "neither in a frigid nor a careless manner," summarized, "This, I say, is the sure and unerring form of worship, which we know that He approves, because it is the form which His word prescribes, and these the only sacrifices of the Christian Church which have His sanction."²²

The *Second London Confession* of the Baptists in paragraph one of its chapter on Scripture states, "The Holy Scripture is the only sufficient, certain, and infallible rule of all saving knowledge, faith, and obedience... which makes the Holy Scriptures to be most necessary, those former ways of God's revealing His will unto His people being now ceased." In its final paragraph of the chapter the Baptists stated, "The supreme judge by which all controversies of Religion are to be determined, and all decrees of councils, opinions of ancient writers, doctrines of man, and private spirits, are to be examined, and in whose sentence we are to rest, can be no other but the Holy Scripture delivered by the Spirit, into which Scripture so delivered, our faith is finally resolved."

We are led to a desire to worship the one true God by the powerful impact of Scripture on the head and the heart. We look to that same word, and it alone, for the manner in which our knowledge of God is increased through the biblical propositions that guide the New Covenant community in its worship.

---

21 *The Library of Christian Classics,* XXIV, ed Geoffrey W. Bromiley (Philadelphia: The Westminster Press, 1953), 93.
22 John Calvin, *The Necessity of Reforming the Church* in *Selected Works of John Calvin,* ed Henry Beveridge and Jules Bonnet (Grand Rapids: Baker Book House, 1983) 1:146, 147.

The freedom given by the principle of *sola scriptura* from human regulations provides the second tension.

The most consistent application of Sola Scriptura is the regulative principle. This is fundamental to the rhythm of worship ensconced in the pattern of revelation/response. Strange would be the serious Christian who purposely would refuse to incorporate any required part of worship or would include something strictly forbidden. "Yes, it is clear that God requires his word to be read," one might reason, "but, seriously, should we really do that every time we get together? It would become a matter of mere ritual." Those words would be incompatible with transparent obedience to truth. If it were to become "mere ritual" that would indicate, not a triviality in the requirement, but a heart problem in pursuing joyful obedience. "Yes, we know that we should pray only to God and allow none to share his glory in sustaining his people," another might observe, "but would it not be an act of genuine gratitude on this Mothers' Day to ask our faithful, but departed, mothers to call our names before Jesus as did the Canaanite woman of Matthew 15?" Calvin's comment about the intercession of the Saints would be an appropriate retort to such a request: "Divine offices are distributed among the saints as if they had been appointed colleagues to the Supreme God." This kind of perversion of biblical requirement and prohibitions would not be a serious threat to a Bible-believing congregation. We hope!

The pressing question, then, is this: "Is there any warrant to include anything in worship that is not clearly stated as a revealed element of corporate worship so long as it is not strictly forbidden?" Could a ballet troupe consisting of the children of church members perform during the giving of the offering, interpreting through the medium of dance the story of the Good Samaritan? Does the Bible specifically forbid this kind of thing; or is it enough that substance in worship always is to give the certain sound of the clear word, an express exposition of that which is revealed? (1 Corinthians 14:6-12)

As something of a precursor to a more full development of the regulative principle, Luther noted, in a criticism of the unwarranted manner in which the Pope's priests conducted worship, "for all worshipping which is not ordained of God or erected by God's word and command, is nothing worth, yea, mere idolatry."[23] John Calvin worked judiciously but zealously to clean out all the superfluities added to worship in the church of the Middle Ages. He observed, "Such is our folly, that when we are left at liberty, all we are able to do is to go astray. And then when once we have turned aside from the right path, there is no end to our wanderings, until we get buried under a multitude of superstitions." To remedy that irresistible tendency of human nature, Calvin set forth a principle of worship known as the regulative principle.

> I know how difficult it is to persuade the world that God disapproves of all modes of worship not expressly sanctioned by His Word. The opposite persuasion which cleaves to them, being seated, as it were, in their very bones and marrow, is, that whatever they do has in itself a sufficient sanction, provided it exhibits some kind of zeal for the honour of God. But since God not only regards as fruitless, but also plainly abominated, whatever we undertake from zeal to His worship, if at variance with His command, what do we gain by a contrary course? The words of God

---

23 Martin Luther, *Tabletalk*, trans. and ed. by William Hazlitt (Fearn, Great Britain: Christian Heritage, 2003), 297.

are clear and distinct, "Obedience is better than sacrifice." "In vain do they worship me, teaching for doctrines the commandments of men," (1 Sam. xv. 22; Matth. xv 9.) Every addition to His word, especially in this matter, is a lie. Mere "will worship" is vanity. This is the decision, and when once the judge has decided, it is no longer time to debate.[24]

In his comments on Psalm 138:2 (*Treasury of David*), Spurgeon made virtually the identical point about God's sole prerogative in the regulation of worship when commenting on the words, "I will worship toward thy holy temple."

> He would worship God in God's own way. The Lord had ordained a centre of unity, a place of sacrifice, a house of his indwelling; and David accepted the way of worship enjoined by revelation. Even so, the true-hearted believer of these days must not fall into the will-worship of superstition, or the wild worship of skepticism, but reverently worship as the Lord himself prescribes. The idol gods had their temples; but David averts his glance from them, and looks earnestly to the spot chosen of the Lord for his own sanctuary. We are not only to adore the true God, but to do so in his own appointed way.

By example in his worship and by precept in his preaching, Spurgeon held fast to the principle that "Christ alone is the law-maker of the church and no rule or regulation in the Christian church standeth for anything unless in its spirit at least it hath the mind of Christ to support and back it up."

---

24 John Calvin, "On the Necessity of Reforming the Church," *Calvin's Selected Works*, ed. and trans. Henry Beveridge (Grand Rapids: Baker Book House, 1983) 1:129.

Though each church must make "necessary regulations as may be made for carrying out our Lord's commands, to meet for worship, and to proclaim the gospel," even such necessary arrangements "are not tolerable if they clearly violate the spirit and mind of Jesus Christ." Christ has not given binding liturgies or legal rubrics. He provides spiritual guidance for his precepts and, if we do not insert our inventions or omit his stated aspects of worship, "he has left us at liberty to follow the directions of his own free Spirit."[25] Scripture-guided worship perfectly illustrates this pattern of form and freedom.

The Puritan Jeremiah Burroughs (1599-1646), a "very amiable divine," who desired to be "free from such mixtures in God's worship,"[26] in the book *Gospel Worship* argued the principle by stating, "All things in God's worship must have a warrant out of God's word, must be commanded; it is not enough that it is not forbidden, and what hurt is there in it? – but it must be commanded. . . . We must all be willing worshippers, but not will worshippers." He then argued from the deaths of Nadab and Abihu, sons of Aaron who offered strange fire, and Uzza, who touched the ark of the covenant, that it was not enough to be sincere, earnest, and willing, nor was inexperience an excuse for unwarranted worship.

Thomas Crosby (1683-1751) set forth the views of Burroughs as those most consistent with the Baptists in their attempts to remove all unbiblical traditions from both their formation of the church itself and their practice of worship. Crosby, the son-in law of Benjamin Keach, having gathered material from the earliest days of the Baptist extension of the

---

25 MTP 14: 617-618

26 Benjamin Brook, *Lives of the Puritans*, (Pittsburgh: Soli Deo Gloria, 1994) 3:18, 20.

Puritan objection to remaining corruptions in the churches, confirmed "the Baptists in their opinion; That the holy scriptures are to be the only rule of our faith and worship; and that we are to practice nothing, as an institution of Christ, which is not therein contained."[27]

History provides an example of the operation of the regulative principle in controversies over church practice. The disagreement between John Bunyan and William Kiffin as to whether an "unbaptized person may be regularly admitted to the Lord's Supper" turned on this. The word "regularly" means precisely, according to the biblical rule. Kiffin showed that the priority of baptism to both church membership and participation in the Lord's Supper was the common acknowledgement of the entire Christian church. The question between them, therefore, was what constitutes Christian baptism? Kiffin argued that only the immersion of a believer was Christian baptism and, therefore, to admit to the Lord's Supper any who had been baptized in infancy violated the biblical requirement for baptism. We have no right to alter God's rules for his church and its proper worship according to the ordinances on the supposition that we are advancing Christian fellowship in so doing. Using the tragic example of Nadab and Abihu "in offering not the same that was commanded," Kiffin stakes his claim of the necessity of not going beyond what Scripture itself, the unerring oracle of God, warranted.

> What shall we say to such as mix their Inventions with the Sacred Institutions and Prescripts of the Great unerring Sovereign: When the same person who is to perform the Obedience, shall dare to appoint the

---

27 Thomas Crosby, *History of the English Baptists*, 4 vols in 2 (Lafayette, TN: Church History Research and Archives, 1978) 1: lx.

Laws? Implying a peremptory purpose of no further observance than may consist with the allowance of his own Judgment? Whereas true Obedience must be grounded on the Majesty of that Power that commands, not on the Judgment of the Subject, or benefit of the Prescript proposed; not so much from the Quality of the things Commanded, as from the Authority of him that Institutes. Is not such a Practice an invasion upon Christ's Prerogative? Do not such men make themselves (as it were) Joynt Authors of his ordinances?[28]

The *Second London Confession* speaking univocally with the *Westminster Confession* stated this principle in chapter 22.

> The light of nature shows that there is a God, who has lordship and sovereignty over all; is just, good and does good to all; and is therefore to be feared, loved, praised, called upon, trusted in, and served, with all the heart and all the soul, and with all the might. But the acceptable way of worshipping the true God, is instituted by himself, and so limited by his own revealed will, that he may not be worshipped according to the imagination and devices of men, nor the suggestions of Satan, under any visible representations, or any other way not prescribed in the Holy Scriptures.

If we have been purified in soul by a sincere obedience to the truth and now pass the time of this present exile in the fitting fear of God (1 Peter 1:17, 22), we cannot possibly

---

28 William Kiffin, *A Sober Discourse of Right to Church-Communion* (London: Printed by George Larkin, 1681) 8th and 9th pages of the preface.

increase either fear or obedience by ignoring what is commanded, employing what is forbidden, or blazing new trails in venturing beyond what God requires. As Kiffin reminds us, God has "never given any such Prerogatives to mankind, as to be Arbitrators how he may be best and most decently Worshiped."[29] We are not wiser than he and we do not increase either the holiness, the joy, or the purity of worship to introduce that which he has not required.

The Regulative Principle provides the third of our tensions to keep us straight.

Scripture-Guided Worship Gives Full Expression to Each of the Three Strands of This Tension.

What is a manner of worship, therefore, or a theory of constructing corporate worship, that will accomplish a scripturally faithful form of worship? How do we conform to the guide of decency and order? How do we maximize the congregation's opportunity to respond to the word? How do we protect ourselves from the tendency to create idols of our own thoughts and creativity? How do we maximize Spirit and truth in the worship of God through Christ?

So, how does one develop a method of planning worship that meets the criterion of form, decency, and order while at the same time avoiding an extraneously mandated, humanly superimposed system of worship? In avoiding a formalized imposition of worship style, is the only option a casual, chatty, cool, and horizontally dominated corporate gathering? The first step, of course, in achieving the beauty of biblical

---

[29] William Kiffin, *A Sober Discourse of Right to Church Communion* (London: George Larkin, 1681) "Preface" 12th page.

integration of form and freedom is to embrace the formal principle of the Reformation, *sola scriptura*. As it did for the Reformers of the sixteenth-century, the principle throws aside barnacleized traditions unwarranted from Scripture and cute immediate innovations indebted to a human quest for novelty. Making a time of worship immediately responsive to the principle of *sola scriptura* involves a careful delineation of scripturally mandated elements of worship integrated into a theologically sound, pastorally sensitive, and Spirit-induced flow of parts creating a wholistic manifestation of praise governed by revelation and infused with grace. The undergirding commitment that maximizes the symmetry of Spirit and truth in worship is the regulative principle.

The regulative principle threatens our haughty evaluations of our creativity. It demotes the glory of our ability to produce worship extravaganzas. Through it we halt in the path of impressive and exciting displays of talent without undercutting the proper stewardship of skill and recognition of true giftedness for the glory of God. We look to the proper execution of both natural and spiritual gifts in submission to divine revelation and God's zeal for his own glory. Through it we crush the quest for human glory and replace that with something of infinitely greater worth. It invites us to experience the beauty and wonder of the entirety of the Word of God. We should not view this principle as something that restricts the expansion of human experience in the worship of God, but as a gift of the imperishable for the perishable. The withering strands of flying grass of a newly mown lawn bear no comparison with the unending fruit coming from the tree of life whose very leaves are set for "the healing of the nations" (Revelation 22:2).

Scripture-guided worship as an expression of the Regulative Principle opens the entire Bible as a guide for worship.

Scripture-guided worship is a serious application of the Regulative Principle. It drives a worship leader to find his source for the content and flow of worship in a biblical passage parallel to that which is the sermonic text for the day. We will illustrate this with one example.

Suppose the text for the day is Acts 17:22-34, Paul's address at the Areopagus. In that passage the theme of creation dominates and spreads its influence all the way to the need for repentance, judgment, righteousness, the incarnation, and resurrection. Phrases in that passage such as "The God who made the world," "being then God's offspring," "He has fixed a day," "judge the world in righteousness," "raising him from the dead," provide so many avenues of connection to other Scriptures that the worship leader should be embarrassed at how much he has to omit. Parallel passages that could serve as a guide to worship in all its parts and provide an exegetical path for the sermon are abundant.

For example, when the biblical revelation begins with, "In the beginning, God created the heavens and the earth" we are introduced to one of the most sublime sources of praise throughout Scripture. Following Genesis 1 as a worship guide powerfully engages Acts 17 and offers the immediate biblical warrant for every element to be included in worship. The refrain, "and God said," along with "God saw that it was good," and "Let us make man in our image," "Be fruitful and multiply," and "I have given you," set themes that never die throughout the biblical corpus. Here we have the suggestion of hymns and songs that praise the omnipotence and wisdom of God. We see immediately that divine revelation provides our knowledge of God and defines our legitimate response. Here we have content for prayers that recognize our dependence on God and offer gratitude for his provision of all things beautiful and nourishing. Our worship in giving becomes truly the recognition that we are only stewards and have nothing that he has not first bestowed so that we may repeat with David, "All things come of thee, and of thine own have we given thee" (1 Chronicles 29:14 KJV). Here we lament that our sin has brought the goodness of this creation to a state of groaning and waiting. Here we recognize that God created all things that he might render his Son altogether lovely in his redemption of sinners and restoration of perfect harmony and unblemished beauty, immutably so, to this creation. Here we find the resonance of Scripture with the hymnic admission, "Were the whole realm of nature mine, that were a present far too small. Love so amazing, so divine, demands my soul, my life, my all."[30]

Other texts abound that would serve as a channel for worshipful understanding. "The heavens declare the glory of God, and the sky above proclaims his handiwork, . . . the law of the Lord is perfect," (Psalm 19:1, 7); "Lift up your eyes on high and see: who created these? He who brings out their host by number, calling them all by name, by the greatness of his might, and because he is strong in power not one is missing," (Isaiah 40:26); "All things were made through him, and without him was not anything made that was made" (John 1:3); "For his invisible attributes, namely, his eternal power and divine nature, have been clearly perceived, ever since the creation of the world, in the things that have been

---

30   Isaac Watts, "When I survey the Wondrous Cross," in *Baptist Hymnal*, hymn # 144.

made. So they are without excuse," (Romans 1:20); "For I consider that the sufferings of this present time are not worth comparing with the glory that is to be revealed to us. For the creation waits with eager longing for the revealing of the sons of God" (Romans 8:19, 20); "To preach to the Gentiles the unsearchable riches of Christ, and to bring to light for everyone what is the plan of the mystery hidden for ages in God who created all things, so that through the church the manifold wisdom of God might now be made known to the rulers and authorities in the heavenly places," (Ephesians 3:8-10); "Worthy are you, our Lord and God, to receive glory and honor and power, for you created all things, and by your will they existed and were created" (Revelation 4:11); "Then I saw a new heaven and a new earth, for the first heaven and the first earth had passed away, and the sea was no more. And I saw the holy city, new Jerusalem, coming down out of heaven from God, prepared as a bride adorned for her husband" (Revelation 21:1, 2); "Since all these things are thus to be dissolved, what sort of people ought you to be in lives of holiness and godliness, waiting for and hastening the coming of the day of God, because of which the heavens will be set on fire and dissolved, and the heavenly bodies will melt as they burn! But according to his promise we are waiting for new heavens and a new earth in which righteousness dwells" (2 Peter 3:11-13).

All over the Bible we are called upon to adore and magnify the God who created all things, for his own glory, for a peculiar purpose, and who will culminate the power and beauty manifest in his intrinsic creative impulse by replacing this fallen order with an everlasting one in which the saints will dwell and praise him forever. Unpacking the elements of worship from this particular doctrinal source expressed in one of a large number of parallel Scriptures gives an orderly guide, exhibits fitting freedom, and conforms precisely to the kind of worship that arises from the text itself. Any of these texts, plus an abundance of others, offers encouragement for praise of God, for prayer, for confession of dependence, for giving, for gratitude, for repentance from attempted autonomy and absence of gratitude, for looking forward to a sinless purified habitation for our glorified bodies in the presence of God forever.

Scripture-guided worship as an expression of the Regulative Principle demonstrates the redemptive coherence of Scripture.

Scripture guided worship proceeds on the assumption that redemption pervades the entire Scripture as a pivotal theme. From the fall of Adam and Eve and *protevangelium* of Genesis 3:15, the Scripture glistens with redeeming love as the most striking attribute implicit in the infinite goodness of God (Deuteronomy 34:6, 7; Psalm 136; John 3:16; John 13:1; John 17:23-26; Romans 5:8; Romans 8:37, 38; Galatians 2:20; Ephesians 2:4; 1 John 4:10, 11; Revelation 1:5). Within the field of attributes that are expressive of the simple, self-existent, and immutable goodness of God we find that Scripture points to justice, holiness, righteousness, faithfulness, wrath, patience, lovingkindness, mercy, grace, and wisdom. These, along with others, are individualized expressions of God's interaction with the finite structures and temporal movements of the created order. Every attribute implies all the others when taken as consistent with God's simple goodness. When we find that the theme of redemption, therefore, runs consistently throughout the Scripture and in itself offers the revelation of all the multifaceted beauty of God, we are confident that any passage that illustrates the divine character also contains material for praise and for looking at the wonder of redeeming love. "For the word of the Lord is upright, and all his work is done in faithfulness. He loves righteousness and justice; the earth is full of the steadfast love of the Lord" (Psalm 33:4, 5).

Scripture guided worship, therefore, witnesses to the doctrinal purpose and coherence of the Bible. The theme of redemption will never be far away from a sermonic text and identical themes will richly adorn numbers of passages throughout the Bible. John 3:16-21 may be supported in worship from the entirety of Psalm 30. Consider the canonical implications of verse 3: "O Lord, you have brought up my soul from Sheol; you restored me to life from among those who go down to the pit." Consider the contrast between eternal life and condemnation in these texts. Look at the reasons for magnifying the attributes of God as displayed in redemption. Contemplate prayers of confession and prayers of gratitude encouraged by the words, "You have turned for me my mourning into dancing; you have loosed my sackcloth and clothed me with gladness" (verse 11). Imagine the powerful fulfillment that seals this to the spirit of the worshipers when they see it reflected in the words, "should not perish but have eternal life" (John 3:16).

The use of a text parallel to the theme of the sermon shows how frequently biblical themes are revisited throughout Scripture and orders the worship in all its essential parts as a direct manifestation of the Regulative Principle. The worship service itself gives an exposition of the parallel text, and at the same gives a thoroughly biblical preparation for the focused exposition of Scripture. Rightly viewed, the Regulative

Principle as unfolded in Scripture-guided worship does not hinder a multitude of ordered but expressive worship experiences; rather, it throws the worship leader, and the congregation, into the big middle of the unfathomable depths of divine revelation and says, "Explore me forever, and never exhaust the sources for offering 'to God acceptable worship, with reverence and awe, for our God is a consuming fire'" (Hebrews 12:28, 29).

Scripture Index

Old Testament

Genesis

1	187
1:28	110
2:3	43
3:15	94, 190
3:21	94
4	109
4:21	91

Exodus

15:1-3	91
15:20-21	111
20:1	40
20:1-2	45
20:8-11	43
20:11	40
31:14-15	44

Leviticus

16:29-34	44
23:24	41
23:32	41
23:39	44

Numbers

15:32-36	44

Deuteronomy

32:1-47	92
32:36	93
34:6-7	190

1 Kings

12:25-33	23
13:34	24

2 Kings

13:4	24
14:24	24
15:18	24
17:21-41	24

1 Chronicles

25	112
25:3	113
25:5-6	113
29:14	188

2 Chronicles

11:13-16	23

Ezra

8:8	62

Nehemiah

7:66-67	62
8:1-3	62

11:20-21	44
13:22	40

Job

38:6-7	110

Psalms

1	2
4:9-11	17
5:9	17
5:10	17
5:12-13	17
10	17
11:16-19	17
15:3-4	17
16:5-7	17
19:1-7	188
19:2-3	10
19:7-14	168
27:4	20
30	191
30:3	191
30:11	191
30:11-12	132
32	93
32:1-2	94
32:2b	94
33:4-5	191
42:11	104
44	104
49	115
49:16-17	132
51	58
57:7-9	105
59:16-17	89
69:29-30	14
69:34	10
84:1	15
84:2	15
84:4	15
87	112
87:7	112
88	104
89	104
89:1	23, 89, 104
89:19-29	23
92	111
105	113
119:130	61
119:169-176	70
135	8
135:5	154
136	190
136:1-26	165
137:2	106
138:2	181
138:4-8	149
138:7	150
138:8	150
139:14-15	11
145	17
145:7	89
146	16, 17
146:1-2	7
150:2	171

Proverbs

11:24	123
12:11	123
13:11	123
13:18	123
13:22	123
14:21	125
14:31	125
21:20	123
22:16	123
22:22-23	123
22:29	123
24:30-34	123
28:22	123

Ecclesiastes	
4:12	171

Isaiah	
11:19	168
40:26	188
43:19-21	15
52:13-15	83
53	83
53	84n5
53:9	83
53:11-12	146
53:12	84
58:13-14	40

Jeremiah	
31:33-34	25

Ezekiel	
36:26-27	25
37:14	25

New Testament

Matthew	
3:1	75, 76
3:13	75
3:15	141
3:17	76
4:1	76
4:13-17	137
4:17	76
4:18	76
5:17	76
5:43-48	76
6:1-4	131
14:33	22
15	179
17:5	21, 76
23:13-15	76
26:26-29	143
26:28	133
28:9	22
28:17	22
28:19	136

Mark	
1:12	76
10:28	76
10:38-39	141
10:38-45	141

Luke	
1:35	139
3:14	76
4:1	76
4:16-19	76
4:17-22	76
4:24-29	76
12:15	123
12:20-21	125
16:1-13	122
19:8-10	123
21:4	129
22	147
22:19	142, 147
24:38-43	157

John	
1:3	188
1:14	21, 29, 157
1:17	29
1:27	76
1:36	76
2:18-22	44
2:19-21	24
3:1-8	44
3:16	190, 191
3:16-21	191
4:19-26	23
4:21-26	44
4:22	24
8:37-44	12
10:7	145
13:1	190
14:6	29
14-16	155
15:1	145
16:14	32
16:14-15	163
17:3-4	139
17:17	27
17:17-19	27
17:19	29
17:23-26	190
18:37	32
20:19	46
20:26-28	157
20:28	159
20:29	46

Acts	
1:10-11	31
2:32-34	155
2:39-41	136
2:41-42	133
2:42	142
4:10-12	50
4:21-24	50
4:34-37	123
5:31	50
5:40-41	50
7:1-4	40
8:12	136
10:47-48	137
16:31-32	137
16:34	137
17	187
17:22-34	187
20:6	41
20:7	37, 42n2, 46
20:16	41
20:28	31

Romans	
1:4	31, 45
1:12	51
1:20	38, 189
1:20-21	43
2:8-9	135
2:13	165
3:13-14	33
5:8	190
5:15	161
5:18-21	58, 166
6:3	133, 140
6:4	138
6:23	166
7:7-12	70
7:10	165
8:1-11	155, 156
8:19-20	189
8:26	167
8:32	140
8:34	167
8:35-36	105
8:37-38	190
10:8-13	134
10:14	3, 57
12:1-2	46
12:5	52

12:12	53	16:1-2	46
12:16	51	16:2	40
14:5	42		
14:5-6a	41		
14:14	42	2 Corinthians	
16:25-27	168	1:17	78
		2:16	77
		2:17	78
1 Corinthians		3:5	77
1:18-25	64	3:6	64
1:21-2:5	80	4:2	28, 78
2:10	163	4:3	78
2:10-13	64	4:4	11
4:1	64	4:6	17
5"4	46	5:11	78
6:19-20	140	5:13	142
6:20	46	8:2	129
9:14	126	8:3	129
9:16	81	8:7	121
10:11	64	9:6	131
10:31	17	10:1-8	55
11	147	11:4-6	55
11:18-20	46	11:8-9	127
11:23-26	147		
11:25	133	Galatians	
11:26-29	143		
12:1-3	55	2:20	190
12:3	134	3:12	165
12:7	26, 138	3:13	46
12:12-13	138	3:13-14	44
14:5	55	3:26-27	141
14:6	114	3:27	139
14:6-12	180	4:4-7	139
14:9-11	28	6:6	127
14:11	28	6:14-16	46
14:12	26		
14:14	55	Ephesians	
14:15-16	53		
14:26	46	1:3-4	167
14:36-38	3, 55	1:4-6	19
14:37-38	65	1:7	148, 166, 167
14:39-40	175	1:22-23	31
15:57	45	2:4	190

2:20	66	2:16	41
3:2-3	63	2:16-23	177
3:8-10	189	2:17	42n2
3:8-11	63	3:16	89, 96, 97
3:17-19	167	3:16-17	3
4:2-3	51	3:16, 17	3
4:4-6	136	4	57
4:5	125	4:16	55, 65
4:7	26		
4:8-13	32		
4:12-13	26	**1 Thessalonians**	
4:12-16	49	1:4-5	78
4:15-16	167	2:4	78
4:25-32	2	2:5	78
4:28	123	2:13	78
4:30-31	26	4:1-8	2
5:18	31	4:9-12	2
5:18-20	26	4:15	64
5:19	89	5:17-18	56
5:20	53		
5:25	31	**2 Thessalonians**	
6:18-20	57	1:11-12	167
		2:9-12	13
Philippians		3:14	65
1:9-11	16	3:17	57
1:19	53		
3:3	44	**1 Timothy**	
3:8-10	142		
3:20-21	148	1:3	80
4:4-9	2	2:1	49, 56
4:6	56	2:2	56
4:8	8	3:15	31
4:14-15	127	3:16	76, 157
4:18	127	4:1-5	177
		4:6	177
Colossians		4:13	62
1:5-7	28	6:2-3	80
1:9-10	28	6:9-10	124
1:13	63	6:17-19	124
1:18	31	6:20	80
2:12	138		
		2 Timothy	

1:13	81	12:28-29	192	
1:14	21	13:5	123	
2:8	29	13:10	27	
2:8-10	168	13:12-15	27	
3:10-16	65	13:15-17	27	
4:2	82	13:20-21	145, 167	
		13:22	62	

Titus

1:3	75
2:1	75
2:7	75
3:8	75

James

1:19-21	51
2:15-17	125
5:4-6	125

Philemon

6	153

Hebrews

1:4	31
1:14	31
2:12	139
2:14-16	31
2:17-18	76
4:9-10	47
4:14-16	47
5:8-9	141
7:26-28	140
7:27	145
9:12-15	145
9:14	31, 137
9:24-28	145
9:28	148
12:2	62
10:1-14	41
10:5-10	146
10:9-10	145
10:14	145
10:18	145
10:20	24
10:23-25	50
10:24-25	42n2, 47

1 Peter

1:1	67
1:8	73
1:12	31, 63
1:13	105
1:17-19	53
1:17-22	184
1:22-25	134
1:25	65
2:9	33
2:9-12	63
2:24	157
3:10	33
5:12	67

2 Peter

1:3	124
1:17	21
1:19	21
3	67
3:11-13	45, 189
3:15-16	67

1 John

1:4	67
2:1-2	167

2:7	68	16:10	68
2:12-14	68	19:6-7	91
3:17-18	125	19:7	31
4:1-3	55	19:10	68
4:2	134	20	69
4:2-3	157	21:1-2	189
4:6-7	55	22	68
4:10-11	190	22:1-5	12
5:13	68	22:2	186
5:14-15	56	22:8	68
5:20-21	159	22:18-19	69

3 John

5-8	128

Jude

3	80

Revelation

1:5	190
4	39
4:8	91
4:10-11	21
4:11	91, 189
5	39
5:8	106
5:8-9	112
5:8-14	90
5:9	90
5:9-10	91
5:12	162
5:12-13	91
5:12-14	21
7:12	91
11:16-18	149
11:17-18	91
13:6	11
14:2	107
15:3-4	91
15:13	91

OTHER TITLES FROM FOUNDERS PRESS

***BY WHAT STANDARD?** God's World ... God's Rules.*
Edited by Jared Longshore

I'm grateful for the courage of these men and the clarity of their voices. This is a vitally important volume, sounding all the right notes of passion, warning, instruction, and hope.

—Phil Johnson,
Executive Director of Grace To You

Truth & Grace Memory Books
Edited by Thomas K. Ascol

Memorizing a good, age-appropriate catechism is as valuable for learning the Bible as memorizing multiplication tables is for learning mathematics.

—Dr. Don Whitney, Professor,
The Southern Baptist Theological Seminary

Dear Timothy: Letters on Pastoral Ministry
Edited by Thomas K. Ascol

Get this book. So many experienced pastors have written in this book it is a gold mine of wisdom for young pastors in how to preach and carry out their ministerial life.

—Joel Beeke, President,
Puritan Reformed Theological Seminary

The Mystery of Christ, His Covenant & His Kingdom
By Samuel Renihan

This book serves for an excellent and rich primer on covenant theology and demonstrates how it leads from the Covenant of Redemption to the final claiming and purifying of the people given by the Father to the Son.

—Tom Nettles, Retired Professor of Historical Theology,
The Southern Baptist Theological Seminary

Strong And Courageous: Following Jesus Amid the Rise of America's New Religion
By Tom Ascol and Jared Longshore

> We have had quite enough of "Be Nice and Inoffensive." We are overflowing with "Be Tolerant and Sensitive." It is high time that we were admonished to "Be Strong and Courageous."
> —Jim Scott Orrick, Author, Pastor of Bullitt Lick Baptist Church

ADDITIONAL TITLES

Wisdom for Kings & Queens: Truth for Life from the Book of Proverbs
By Jared Longshore

Still Confessing: An Exposition of the Baptist Faith & Message 2000
By Daniel Scheiderer

By His Grace and for His Glory
By Tom Nettles

Getting the Garden Right
By Richard C. Barcellos

The Law and the Gospel
By Ernie Reisinger

Teaching Truth, Training Hearts
By Tom Nettles

Coming in 2021

Just Thinking: About the State
By Darrell Harrison and Virgil Walker

The Transcultural Gospel
By E.D. Burns

Ancient Gospel, Brave New World
By E.D. Burns

Galatians: He Did It All
By Baruch Maoz

Missions by the Book
By Chad Vegas and Alex Kocman

Baptist Symbolics Vol. 1
For the Vindication of the Truth: A Brief Exposition of the First London Baptist Confession of Faith
By James M. Renihan

Order these titles and more at press.founders.org

Made in the USA
Middletown, DE
27 April 2023

29542937R00119